THE WAY TO CHRIST

THE WAY TO CHRIST

Spiritual Exercises

POPE JOHN PAUL II
Karol Wojtyla

Translated by Leslie Wearne

HarperSanFrancisco
A Division of HarperCollins*Publishers*

FIRST HARPERCOLLINS PAPERBACK EDITION PUBLISHED IN 1994.
ISBN 0-06-064216-5 (pbk)

An Earlier Edition of This Book Was Cataloged As Follows:
John Paul II, Pope.
THE WAY TO CHRIST
Translation of: Rekolekcje, do mlodziecy akademickiej.
1. Spiritual exercises. I. Title.
BX2187.P6J6413   1984   248.3   83-48426
ISBN 0-06-064204-1 (cloth)

---

94 95 96 97 98 RRD (H) 10 9 8 7 6 5 4 3 2 1

This edition is printed on acid-free paper that meets the American National Standards Institute Z39.48 Standard.

Contents

Translator's Preface

Pope John Paul II's lifelong concern for the formation and education of the young is well known. The two retreats found in the present volume represent practical examples of this concern from the period immediately prior to the Second Vatican Council, when he was auxiliary Bishop of Cracow (1962), and from the immediately post-conciliar period, when he was Archbishop of the city and had already been made Cardinal (1972).

Of course such pastoral work had become particularly important in Poland because of the fact that the State had taken over the task of education, suppressing religious teaching in the schools and universities of the country, and aiming at the imposition of atheism in all areas of society and culture. However, the questions dealt with are of deep interest to other societies as well: human dignity, the work ethic, the condition of women, atheism, and so on. This volume can therefore be of help to people who want to reflect once again, maybe in a slightly different perspective from that with which they are familiar, on the practical application and contemporary relevance of the fundamental truths of the faith.

These two retreats were preached in the old church of Saint Anne, in the heart of the university section of Cracow. It should be remembered that they were not given from written texts, but were tape-recorded on the spot and then transcribed by some of the young people who flocked in increasing numbers to hear their bishop speak. These transcriptions were then edited for the Polish edition (*Do Mlodziecy Akademickiej*) by Father Andrzey Bardecki and Miss Irena Kinaszewska. In 1982 the Vatican Press published a re-edited Italian version (translated by Fathers Carmelo Giarratana and Stanislaw Slabon) under the title *Esercizi spirituali per i giovani*. The present English translation has been made from the Italian version, although the longer Polish original has been consulted on certain points.

In the first retreat, which I call "The Image of God Within" (in the Italian version, "God, Man and Religion"), emphasis is placed on God's movement toward human beings to help them to rediscover, in their full human freedom, their original truth and greatness; our turning to God and our witness before others are seen as the two elements of our human response to this movement on God's part. (The word *witness* is a sort of constant in both retreats, and is seen as meaning both believing in Christ in communion, and also carrying out one's own specific task in the Christian community and in society in general. The author also points out the need to allow ourselves to be filled with the "word" until it becomes "flesh" and reveals the Word, the Son of God.)

In the second retreat, which I call "Christ Within Us" (in the Italian version, "The Path of the Christian"), the whole sacred character and beauty of the prayer-life which unites us to God is thrown into clear relief, with the sacraments of Penance and the Eucharist emphasized as the vital and indivisible means to forgiveness and communion.

*   *   *

English lends itself less to a rhetorical style than do Polish and Italian, so that I have had to simplify certain turns of phrase, eliminating a large amount of repetition where this was used simply for emphasis. Since the present text will be read, rather than be spoken out loud, I have tried to produce a text which reads more easily and is therefore slightly more literary, but which still retains some of the immediate flavor of the spoken language.

These retreats were preached in 1962 and 1972—that is, respectively over twenty and ten years ago—and I have made no attempt to up-date them in any way, since a part of their interest undoubtedly lies in their value as historical documents: it is interesting to know what the man who is now Pope was saying, and how he was expressing his thoughts, in previous periods of his life.

As concerns specific points of translation, the main problem is with the word *czlowiek*, which is usually translated into English as *man*; however, in Polish (as in, for instance, German) this word has no sexist connotations and is not the same word as that used for *man* as opposed to *woman*. I have translated this word variously, according to context, as *the person* (in places where there was no risk of philosophical confusion), *human beings, man*, or simply *we*. Another problem is that the author talks about the *I* or *ego*, and, in order to avoid any Freudian overtones, I have used the word *self*, or have sometimes said "the self or *I*" if I felt further clarification was needed.

I have used the Revised Standard Version of the Bible for Scripture quotations, occasionally taking a word or two from some other translation in order to fit in with the Polish version used by the author. All the footnotes, and also the majority of Scripture references in the text, have been added by me.

L. W.

Part One:

The Image of God Within

A retreat for university students
Cracow, 1962

1. God Is Person

It will be helpful if we begin with the simple observation that we are gathered together here, and then consider what this means.

Let us ignore external interpretations which give us answers connected with fideism and tradition, and instead follow that interior voice which springs from our consciences and convictions.

What, then, is the meaning of our presence here? It stems from the fact that we have within us a specific interior need which has brought us here. We cannot explain what this need is if we do not accept that each one of us has an interior life or inner person: we do not consist only of an exterior or outer person, but also of an interior person.

So the need which has brought us here comes from within, from the interior person, and belongs to our soul. The inner person is seeking, and if it is to be successful in its search and find what it seeks, it must engage in interior recollection, in which it operates according to different rhythms and methods from those of the outer person. A retreat is principally a matter of recollection—not quantitative recollection, but first and foremost interior recollection.

Our presence here is therefore not only a result of tradition, a certain impulse or some atavistic instinct. Of course a large part is played by tradition, as made up of "facts" which we inherit from experience as a whole; there are many, many different lived experiences of Christianity, Catholicism and the Church; we feel our link with them, and that is why we are here. The experience which brings us here is also very personal and consists in the need of the interior person.

This is significant in an age where it would seem that the whole destiny of the person and of his existence must be guided and directed from outside, with external means—that is, with the use of methods and means produced by people. This is happening in our particular age, when man's marvelous accomplishments are without parallel in the past—or at least so far as we know. However, even in this era, where people want to plan man's whole destiny and existence from outside with the help of technical means provided by so-called civilization, the person comes to realize that everything he produces and creates outside himself cannot be compared with himself and that he cannot stand outside himself. Inside, we are ourselves, and this basic and constant awareness of the existence of the interior self or soul gives rise within us to the need for fulfillment, which is why we have come on this retreat.

The reason we have come is to observe our own self with care and attention. Let us carefully observe our self in different situations and activities; let us constantly examine and observe our self, I should say, in view of its vital and absolute importance.

We come here to examine our self, and not only for the importance it has, for example, in relation to the proper development or running of a certain laboratory or office or occupation (including cooking and housework); in these cases the self has only a relative or functional importance. However, the self also has its own absolute importance. If we come on retreat, the aim is to examine our self under the aspect of absolute importance.

I should like to explain the difference between relative and absolute importance with the help of a very ordinary example; for you it will already be a part of the past, since it refers to high school days. Sometimes a student will solve some very difficult problem in class, and this is an important moment for him; then at the end of class, the students start playing ball and the one who solved the problem so brilliantly now shows no aptitude at all for the game, while another manages to shine and show his importance. These are two examples of relative importance. The different moments of relative importance in my past constantly shift; in the example we saw that while one person is important in one field, another is important in a different one. We receive continuous information on such aspects of relative importance. We are constantly informed of outstanding human achievements in the field of sport—and maybe somewhat less so in the field of science. (To avoid any misunderstanding, I would hasten to add that I am very interested in sport and, indeed, that I am just as interested in sport as I am in science.) We are constantly kept up to date as regards sport, science and technology, and we share in these moments of relative importance for mankind—a gold or silver medal, a cosmonaut, and so on. All these things refer to the aspect of relative importance.

However, we have come here with another attitude and a different aim: that of seeking what is important in an absolute sense. This is of real interest. We are here as a group, but we are not an undifferentiated mass. There is no gathering in which each one of us is more wholly himself and has a fuller sense of his own selfhood and his own absolute importance than he has here. So what we want to do is to examine our self with care and attention under the aspect of its absolute importance.

In human beings this awareness is linked to their rela-

tionship with God. You may be surprised at this, but I
would ask you to look at yourselves carefully, especially in
moments of personal prayer. Every time we enter into contact with God we rediscover our self in its absolute importance. This rediscovery is of course not always simple or
easy or, let us say, clear. Our prayer is sometimes mechani-
cal and superficial, and with our experience and knowledge
we do not even manage to glimpse the essence of our search
for our personal self or discover it in its absolute importance
through our relationship with God. And this is why we are
here on retreat.

If we try to deny a person's relationship with God (which
is very deep and secret, but still very real), then human life
splinters into the myriad problems of relative importance.
This is the way the interior life of the individual disinte-
grates, but the collective life of mankind and humanity is
destroyed in the same way. Outside the relationship with
God, the life of the individual and of mankind does not
reach the unity and wholeness which only this relationship
can bring. All this may seem rather strange and complicated
to you. However, I would beg you to reflect on it. Sometimes we express this idea by saying that our life loses its
meaning when it is separated from the relationship with
God; we shall talk about this tomorrow.

Humanity has a tendency to ignore the reality of this situation and attribute a meaning to its own life outside the
relationship with God. These two tendencies struggle for
the supremacy in human life, both in that of the individual
and in that of mankind as a whole.

It is symptomatic that when the person sets God aside
and tries to base his own life and that of others on something outside the relationship with God, he also tries to attribute absolute importance to various objects which in fact
have only relative value and importance. We can say that

he absolutizes them and raises them to the absolute level.

We all know the Ten Commandments. The first has always been, "You shall have no other gods besides me." We often repeat this commandment when praying or carrying out an examination of conscience, and on other occasions, and we wonder about its historical or prehistorical basis. It had contemporary relevance at the time when the Israelites found themselves in the midst of pagans who worshipped a number of divinities and when they themselves made the golden calf and worshipped it. And it is just as relevant today: it is simply that the idols have changed!

It is significant that those same atheists who struggle to "free" human life from the relationship with God also, albeit unconsciously, introduce a wide variety of contemporary idols into human life and consciousness. They are not golden idols called Baal or Astarte, like those we read about in the Old Testament; they are more abstract idols. They have only relative value and importance, but are given absolute importance as if they were God. The history of culture and thought has known many of these divinities.

Progress: this is the connecting thread; it is a very positive and valid thing, but when it is raised to the level of divinity and given absolute, rather than relative, significance, then it is no longer in its correct place. Physical objects can also become idols, and it would seem that this is the case with the atom today. Sometimes a similar absolute importance is given to a people or race. It would seem that there is a sort of built-in nemesis, or in fact something deeper than that, in this tendency: when man gives absolute importance to something which has only relative importance, after a certain amount of time he starts, so to speak, to avenge himself or exact retribution from himself and immediately overthrows whatever he had previously raised up to the dignity of God.

My dear children, reflect well on the first divine commandment: "You shall have no other gods besides me." From the perspective of this commandment, carefully consider the facts and examine your own self and your soul.

We come on retreat in order to discover and analyze our own self and examine it from the perspective of its absolute importance, that is, in its relationship with God. A retreat is an interior and religious matter. There is a current of thought which reasons as follows: religion is a human product, inasmuch as humanity has created a god for itself. And why has it created him? In order to submit to him—in other words, to submit to its own product. This is known as alienation.

Humanity undoubtedly does create the *concept* of God. Like other concepts, we have created this one on the basis of personal analysis of the facts, and such analysis has often wrongly understood and undervalued the facts themselves. Man created a concept of God for himself because he did not understand the forces of nature and put God in their place. It is clear that two orders are being confused here: the first or primary causal order is being confused with what we call that of second or secondary causes. For a long time we did not recognize all the multitude of secondary causes— and we undoubtedly still do not do so, although we are constantly investigating them in ever greater depth. In any case, knowledge of the closer and more immediate secondary causes certainly does not eliminate the problem of the first cause. It is said that knowledge of God is not scientific, and we often act on this assumption. You must forgive me for dwelling on this matter, but I know that your minds are constantly exercised by it. I want to move on as soon as possible from this subject to the question of life and the response to life; however, a certain amount of prior clarification and reflection is necessary.

When one examines some subject "scientifically," this is

taken as referring to one specific way of thinking; this is the method normally used by the natural sciences. Even so, there are other ways of thinking. However, this is a vast question and we cannot study it in detail here.

In this connection it would be helpful to read something of Gilson's brief work *God and Philosophy*.* This is not an easy text to grasp, but it does have the advantage of brevity. We often try to read such books, only to exclaim almost at once: "I can't understand it!" And the reason we do not understand is that we are accustomed to thinking in a certain way. We do understand for a moment, but then we lose our train of thought. However, I want to say at once that our scientific and intellectual approach to God takes place in very simple stages. All human thought in every branch of science moves through these stages: we start by experiencing something and then set out to seek the causes.

This happens spontaneously even in the mind of a child, who experiences something and asks: "Why?" Thus our scientific and methodological search for God as first cause follows the same path. We do not create the idea or concept of God from nothing; we create it—and rightly so—on the basis of external facts and the reality of the visible world, but also on the basis of interior reality. A combination of the two undoubtedly provides the starting point for our movement toward God. When I think of God, I am turning to him because I see the world with my own eyes; this is the simplest and most elementary experience. However, when I think of God, this is also because I have an interior self. Only that *I* thinks *God*. Only that *I* can think of *God*.

God exists. Although it may sometimes be rather vague, we do, despite everything, have the concept and conviction

*Etienne Gilson, *God and Philosophy* (New Haven: Yale University Press, 1941); this book is a collection of lectures given by Gilson at the University of Indiana in 1940.

of God's existence. We may not have examined this line of reasoning in its full depth, and some people may also object that it is not scientific. By "in its full depth" I mean to the level of our common intelligence, in other words, that of myself as physicist, historian and theologian.

So when I think of God I am usually thinking of the Creator. However, First Cause and Creator are not the same thing. When I think of the First Cause I am thinking in abstract terms, but when I think of the Creator I am thinking in much more concrete or specific terms. Let us examine the concept of "Creator" for a moment. We can go back to our catechism, which says: "To create means to make something out of nothing." However, this is not the best definition. When we say "to make" we think of a person making something, but the concept of the Creator who is, in his essence, the First Cause is something different. Creator, God, he who is.

See if you can find a copy of *He Who Is* by the English author Eric Mascall.* God said to Moses: "I am who I am"—he whose essence is "who is." Do any of us creatures have "isness," or existence, as our essence?

Creating undoubtedly does mean making something out of nothing, but in the more specific sense of giving existence—not constructing objects or beings, but transmitting existence, causing a being to begin existing outside myself. This is what the Creator does.

God is Creator. My dear children, we make a retreat in order to examine our own self specifically in the perspective of its absolute importance. I said that what is of absolute importance in me is linked with God. This is why I am now saying that God is the Creator, because we have this concept of God within ourselves.

---

*Eric Mascall, *He Who Is: A Study in Traditional Theism* (Hamden, CT: Shoe String Press, 1970).

We come on retreat to examine our self, to examine with attention and care the image of God which is found within us. A retreat is a wonderful thing, and you must remain faithful in making it.

Maybe the greatest obstacle for us in our relationship with God, who is Creator, is the fact that he is invisible, and we wish he were the object of direct experience. However, it is easy to realize that if he were the object of direct experience and were visible, he would not be God. God cannot be visible. Matter is visible. The body is visible, and we know that it is not God; it is destroyed, dies, changes, dissolves. It is subject to time, whereas God is eternity. He is above time and knows no beginning and no end. God is outside the concepts of beginning and end; they do not refer to him, but they are found in the world of created things; beginning and end are found in me.

He is invisible, and this is something very special. However, if I look within myself and reflect on myself for a moment I can say that to a significant degree I too am invisible. The visible aspect of myself, which can be perceived by the senses, is only a part of me; we might describe it as the outer person, whereas the inner person is invisible. So the inner person, who is invisible, cannot be in conflict with God, who is also invisible. I come into contact with God within my mind and soul. My mind is invisible!

My dear children, the aim of a retreat is to examine the image of God which we have within us. And what image of God do I carry in my mind and in my soul? The word *image* has many meanings. So the aim of the retreat is to examine one's own self in the perspective of its absolute importance and also to examine with care the image of God in one's own mind and soul. What is God's image in me like? I am put in mind of a scrap of conversation I heard between two children. One asked the other who she thought God was, and she replied that maybe he was strength, or maybe light. Clearly these were metaphors, but what is significant is that these two children wondered about this point and that they were seeking some answer. This is how our interior intellect studies and seeks the image of God within us.

A retreat has the aim of finding this image in its fullness. We must reflect on the image of God as found in each one of us; otherwise this study of our own self would be meaningless and would degenerate into consideration of various things of only relative value, and then this would not be a retreat. So I urge you from now on to seek the image of God within yourselves. This image may be very poor or clouded; or it may be unclear and fragmentary because your search for God lacks constancy. There may be a certain superficiality and a lack of depth and interior life and union in your knowledge of God.

Thus a retreat should heighten our interiority. However, my dear children, this also involves a search for one's own self and for the basis of its most essential value—that is, for what is of absolute importance in it.

I realize that in today's reflection I have not answered the main question. Indeed, although you may think I have done so, I have in fact not replied at all. However, I tell you that I have not answered the question of why I recognize my self in its absolute importance only in the encounter with God. I want to answer this question tomorrow. For today, let us say that this happens inasmuch as God is not solely strength or light. God is Person. Only the encounter with that Person who is God provides us, or our self, with the sense of the absolute importance of life.

Amen

2. Christianity, the Religion of Choice

Today I want to talk about the Gospel or, in other words, about revelation.

Our first impression may be that the Gospels are simply a book, and this is the form in which we hold it in our hands, read it with our eyes and hear its words with our ears. The Church systematically proclaims sections of the Gospels to us day by day at Mass; sometimes these readings are long and sometimes short.

It is truly a unique book. It has by now been translated into almost every language in the world and even into various dialects, but it loses nothing of its initial freshness and even a certain Semitic flavor. This regional flavor, which is derived from the fact that Jesus taught in Aramaic and lived in Palestine, in no way diminishes its universality. Its unique content strikes and affects people everywhere.

Even so, the Gospels are a great problem. There is maybe no other book which has had its authenticity or veracity tested under every aspect; and new research continually confirms its authenticity and veracity.

In the past the method primarily used by biblical scholars who studied the Gospels was that of philological exegesis, examining them from a linguistic viewpoint. Today there are other methods, one of the most important of which is archeology; and excavations also confirm the truth of Sacred Scripture. There is a book which has been translated into Polish under the title *The Bible Was Right** and in which the author shows, text by text, how the events of the Old and New Testaments are confirmed by the research and conclusions of modern historical and archeological science.

We usually approach the Gospels not just as a book but as a collection of news items, and we often compare the information found in Sacred Scripture with that provided by science. (Thus, for example, in the case of the vexed question of human evolution, that is, the origins of man, people still argue passionately against the scientific view, basing themselves on information from the Bible. Even so, the tension around this question has eased somewhat of late.) This type of comparison and argument focuses clearly on the Bible as a collection of information. So, inasmuch as the Gospels are part of the Bible, and specifically of the New Testament, they are a collection of information. If the Bible is a collection of information given to us by God, we are trying to refute it with conclusions reached by the human intellect.

When we examine the information found in the Bible from the historical and scientific viewpoint, we come to realize that there is maybe no other written work which constitutes as great a problem as the Gospels do. No other literary work—not even the works of Homer or Shakespeare or any of the greatest classics of literature—has given rise to such conflict. Such an atmosphere of tension, struggle, doubt and conviction has not been created around any work other than the Gospels.

At the beginning I said, "Gospel, or, in other words, revelation." If we consider and read the Gospels solely as a collection of information, albeit religious information (and I

---

*This popular book by Werner Keller was published in the United States under the title *The Bible as History* (New York: Morrow, 1956).

need not repeat that it is natural, historical and religious information, but will simply say that it is information about God), we are not studying it in depth and we shall not even scratch the surface of its real nature or essence.

"Gospel, or, in other words, revelation." It is not simply a collection of information or a scientific monograph. Monographs define certain facts, truths and views, but they do not express the person; their authors do not speak to us of themselves or bare their souls to us. On the other hand, the Gospels are true self-revelation. God reveals or opens himself to man, and if we do not understand and interpret the Gospels in this sense, it means that we are not approaching them in proper depth.

God speaks to us of himself, but not like a journalist. It is impossible to speak of oneself with the detachment of a journalist. God speaks of himself in such as way that he is found within this information. In the Gospels, the most important thing is not the words but the content or reality. It is clearly a form of written language, but language used simply as a means to reveal this reality to us: God speaks of himself.

We talked about God yesterday also. However, we were talking about him according to human categories, approaching the search for him with human means. Let us cast our minds back to yesterday's talk, when we said that, although it may be correct, the expression *First Cause* tells us less about God than the expression *Creator* does.

In the Gospels God speaks of himself, telling us and revealing to us who he is—who he is in his divinity and deepest reality. He says that he is love and tells us how he is love. He is love because he is Father, Son and Holy Spirit, and in this way he is, in himself, love.

Further, not only does he speak of himself, but through the Gospels he tells us what he wants. He tells us what he wants *from* us, but first and foremost he tells us what he wants *for* us, and this is why he tells us who he is and says that he is love. He says that he wants to draw each and every one of us into this love and involve us in it. This is both a great self-revelation and a great offer!

God speaks of himself to each and every person. He says that he is forgiveness. Only in the world of the Gospels do we encounter forgiveness. It is maybe difficult to find a text which can speak to us better about God under this aspect. How realistic the parable of the prodigal son is! And this is not a literary realism but an existential one. The Gospels are not a description of God. In them, God *is*.

If we study the Gospels in depth or at least try to do so, we find a twofold reality: God, in the person of Jesus Christ, is present in them, so that they are not only a description of his life, but an encounter with the Christ who lives, speaks, acts, suffers, dies and rises again. If we read the Gospels in depth we will also find what we call *grace*. Imagine that someone reveals himself to you in this way, opening himself and speaking to you like this; if this took place between one person and another we should call it grace or, better still, a gift.

Let us consider what God says and what he wants to give me. He wants to draw me into his love and enfold me in himself—and he is love itself. He wants to give himself to me. This is very wonderful.

It is not enough simply to read the Gospel. Maybe you think that I am going to say that we must live it, but even that would not be enough. We must have an encounter in the Gospel—yes, an encounter. Any way of approaching or studying it, however careful, exegetical or scientific it may be, will be self-defeating if it does not bring about such an encounter. We may ask whom we must meet in the Gospel. Yesterday we said that God is Person. This is the Person we find in the Gospel. We must have a personal encounter with him in the Gospel, and this is something absolutely new. It is not simply an idea about God, but is something absolutely new.

In the Gospels God is the second self, the divine self, and my self and this divine self meet. God is the second self and thus he is *Thou*. This is how we must speak to him. Christ taught us to address him as *Thou*, as *Father*, always using the familiar form of address: *Thou* art in heaven; *Thy* name; *Thy* kingdom; *Thy* will. This *Thou* is the second self.

This is why I say that the Gospel must entail an encounter, that we must meet with him; for him I am *thou* and for me he is *Thou*. If this encounter has not taken place, you have not yet read the Gospel.

It is the word of God addressed to humanity. However, it is not simply a sermon or a speech or a collection of random words. It is an interior word, which looks for a response from each one of us; and our response must be a choice for him. Christ does not only teach us to address God as *Thou*, which is an unequivocal term expressing intimacy. No, in the Gospel Christ calls us to choose God.

There is an old hymn in which we sing: "We choose God, we long for God, we want God. . . ." To want is to choose, to choose God who is in the Gospel, and choosing this God means choosing Christ, because God reveals himself in him. Choose Christ, because you see, my dear children, Christianity is not an abstract religion, but the religion of the choice of Christ. This means being baptized. Baptism means having chosen Christ.

I choose Christ. Christianity is the religion of choice, of the choice of God in Christ. The external expression of this choice of God in Christ means professing our faith. I choose God in the act of acknowledging him. I do not think of him simply in an abstract way like an idea. I choose God through the very fact of acknowledging him. Christ spoke about this in clear terms, emphasizing the importance of this confession when he said: "Every one who acknowledges me before men"—*before men*—"I also will acknowledge before my Father who is in heaven; but whoever denies me before men, I also will deny before my Father who is in heaven" (Matthew 10:32; cf. Luke 12:8). He did not say this as a stern judge, but from his position as Christ, thinking of the necessary condition of our response to God and choice of God. It is not possible to choose God continuously without recognizing, or acknowledging, him.

People today often say that religion is a private or personal matter. However, there are limits to the private and personalized nature of this matter of the religion of Christ. One limit is set by our duty and right to the public confession of God, since confessing him means acknowledging to others that one is on God's side. It does not necessarily mean beating drums and blowing trumpets and repeating oneself obsessively; it simply means acknowledging that one is on his side when circumstances call for such acknowledgment. The test of faith is always based on such public profession.

Jesus wanted the man to whom he entrusted the Church in a special way, the Apostle Peter, to undergo the test of faith, and this test of faith consisted of acknowledging that he was with Christ. And we know that at the critical moment Peter did no acknowledge that he was with Christ: "I do not know the man" (cf. Matthew 26:69–75). Later he repented and acknowledged that he was with him, confessing it even when this would entail persecution, imprisonment and death.

Christianity is the religion of our choice of God. Choosing God, or choosing Christ, means in some way choosing oneself, choosing one's own self in a new way. We are convinced that being Christians means in some way choosing ourselves. It means a type of existence, a foundation, a life-style and a specific morality.

I am mentioning this matter only briefly now because, as I said, this concerns the human content of the Gospel and I want to devote tomorrow's talk specifically to this subject; but let me devote today's talk to the divine aspect of the Gospel.

Choosing oneself undoubtedly means choosing God and Christ. I would also add that, if this were not so, Christ would not have said such things as: "I was hungry and you gave me no food, I was thirsty and you gave me no drink, . . . naked and you did not clothe me." *Me*. Who is this *me*? Him, always him. When did we not do this to him? "As you did it not to one of the least of these, you did it not to me." (Cf. Matthew 25:41–46.)

Thus, the Gospel comes to us as a possibility or choice. We must choose God in Christ.

However, there is also the possibility of refusing God. It sounds horrifying, but it is true that I, a person, can refuse God. Human history is full of examples of this. The Gospel is not the only active force in the lives and actions of humanity and in those of each individual; parallel with it and in opposition to it there is a second force which I would call the antigospel.

The antigospel maybe has its origins in the words uttered at the beginning of human history: "You shall be as gods" (Genesis 3:5). Now, in the history of mankind and of each individual person—in one's own personal history—this antigospel, this opposite of the Gospel, takes on certain individual or collective forms, with constantly new expressions. Thus we are living in the toils of a contemporary expression or formulation of this antigospel. We see it in and around us; we feel it, read about it and recognize it. It is to be found everywhere.

The antigospel has two main characteristics. The first is that in the antigospel the primacy of matter—of material things, things which are of this world and are rooted in economic considerations—is constantly reiterated. Man is placed in subservience to matter, which is seen as governing everything and shaping people's actions in an absolute manner. The second element of this antigospel is the belief that freedom is an end in itself. The Gospel states that freedom tends toward love. One is free in order to do good, that is, to love. The antigospel states that freedom is an end in itself. In this way it eliminates love and the possibility of love in human life and in interpersonal relations. (I shall give more detailed consideration to this question when dealing with the human content of the Gospel.) If man is dominated by the means, to what extent can he himself be the end, and how can his freedom become the end?

In the world of the antigospel there is no place for forgiveness, no place for the parable of the prodigal son, because the world of the antigospel has no Father.

Like the Gospel, the antigospel is not an abstract force. It is something within each one of us, and we are constantly engaged in an interior struggle with it.

There is one last problem. We know that the Gospel ends with Christ's passion—with the cross. Although his passion and death are in fact followed by the resurrection, the cross is still seen as the symbol of Christ and the Gospel.

Christ himself explained why he died on the cross, and we find this explanation in every catechism. Remember the fourth of the six truths of the faith: "The Son of God became man, and died on the cross to redeem us and save us for all time." And Christ said: "God so loved the world that he gave his only Son, that whoever believes in him should not perish but have eternal life" (John 3:16). And this is the answer: Christ died on the cross for love—for love of mankind.

However, Christ died on the cross to satisfy a requirement of justice too. Earlier on, while he was still traveling about Palestine, teaching and working miracles, he spoke of this requirement: "The Son of man must be betrayed into the hands of sinners" (Mark 14:41). He died to meet the requirements of justice in God's regard, which demanded this sacrifice. This was because we are sinners before God and have no justification before him.

Can we be justified in remaining silent before the word of God? Is it not unjustified to close ourselves (as we sometimes do totally) in the face of what we are offered in divine revelation? Anybody who states that God does not exist, even though he is the very source of existence, cannot claim to be justified before God.

You may say that we do not know, that we cannot know; and of course you are in a sense right. When Christ was dying on the cross he said: "Father, forgive them, for they know not what they do" (Luke 23:34). "They know not." But he knew! And this is why justice was necessary and indispensable for him. Ransom had to be paid and redemption brought about, in order to restore the balance; he had to place himself between the first *I* or divine Self and the second *I* or our self.

Those who respond with indifference to God's love are surely not blameless in his regard. And this is why Christ is necessary. His crucifixion is needed in order to bring the various forces and relationships into balance. There is something wonderful, but also overwhelming, in these words of God in the Gospel, in this self-opening, self-manifestation and self-giving of the divine Self for mankind! This is all the more so if we consider how halting our re-

sponse is and how we very often prefer to avoid it altogether and not listen to God or answer him. "Don't speak to
me!" is our attitude. This is why Christ is needed in his position on the cross—and forever.

We Christians, members of the religion of choice and of
the Church, have heard all this, thus "fixing" Christ in this
position.

If this is the divine content of the Gospel, what is required of us? Is it enough to keep Christ in that position?
No, my dear children; we must all take up our position beside him.

Christianity is the religion of choice, and it is a difficult
and demanding choice, particularly when the forces of the
antigospel have the upper hand. This choice is difficult and
demanding, but it is also full of significance.

Contemporary Catholicism acquires a special importance
if we consider the difficulties entailed in our choice and in
our witness to Christ.

We may ask what is required of us, living as we do in an
age when it seems that injustice in God's regard has become
almost systematic. God is existence, but people say that he
does not exist. He is love and they are indifferent toward
him—and they are careful not to waken the human heart
from this indifference.

However, God has his ways.

With the sacrament of Confirmation we become witnesses; and a witness is not simply a conventional figure
but is a person who testifies to Christ. A witness is an adult
Christian, adult in conviction, in experience and in fidelity
to Christ. Most of those present have been confirmed. We
are witnesses to Christ by conviction and experience. This is
our position.

At this point I should like to speak more specifically of
the Mother of Christ.

Apart from the Gospel and the antigospel there is also the protogospel. When God first revealed his plan for the incarnation of his Son, he spoke to the serpent about the Mother of God: "I will put enmity between you and the woman, and between your seed and her seed; she will bruise your head" (Genesis 3:15).*

Christianity means being with Christ, in descending from her! This is not simply a devotional matter, concerning a certain type of religiosity in which we give great honor to Mary, the Mother of Jesus. Here we are talking about being descended from her.

She was with Christ at his birth and also at his death. Thanks to Mary we are with Christ. Through her, as her descendants; hers and his; his and hers. "She will bruise your head, and you will bruise her heel."

Amen

*The author accepts the reading of the Vulgate; the Hebrew text says, "*He* shall bruise your head."

3. The Human Person

The Gospel has a deeply human content. Although on the one hand it is the manifestation and word of God, on the other it was written totally by people.

The human content of the Gospel is primarily bound up with Christ, who lives a human life in the Gospel. If we leave his divinity, his divine mission and the miraculous aspect—everything about him which is superhuman and extraordinary—aside for one moment, we can see his life as truly human and ordinary. It is quite remarkable that the one aspect does not diminish or detract from the other but that they are mutually complementary and form one homogeneous whole. The divine content of the Gospel is bound up with the person of Christ, just as the human content is, even though the latter is obviously linked to the presence of all the people we find around him in the Gospel.

Christ's human life is truly human in every way. He is rightly taken as the model for human life and the solution of our problems, not only those concerned with deeper matters, but also those concerned with normal routine matters.

We are often faced with the very simple and elementary question of what we should be doing with our lives. We can find the answer in the Gospel, by looking at Jesus Christ. This is why I said that Christ is a model for us. If it were possible to summarize an answer to the question, "What should I do with my human life?" the answer we should find in Christ would probably be along the following lines: "I should do what Christ did with his human life. He lived it wholly in service and love, filling his whole life with love and service." When we summarize the human content of the Gospel in this way, it helps make our reply much clearer.

The Gospel undoubtedly has a deeply human content, and today's talk is primarily concerned with analyzing this content, in order to pinpoint certain fundamental "positive" aspects which we find in Christ's human life and which can be found in the lives of each one of us.

If we look at the human life of Christ our Lord, we can each of us put him in our place without difficulty. He is a universal model because each person can put Christ in his or her place and live his or her life as he led his human life, according to the same principles, devoting it wholly to service and love.

In this perspective, let us try to define certain basic positive aspects of every human life.

Today people often talk—especially in psychology—about the dangers of frustration, that is, the loss of a sense of value. It is described as an unsatisfied or unfulfilled need or desire, so that a situation is created within the person which damages or shatters the personality—even if only in part or under only one aspect.

The danger of frustration is always present where there is no system of reference to higher values, which would make it impossible. It must be recognized that in the present age this danger hangs over each person because of the lack of a higher system of values to which to refer one's hopes and one's mind, and particularly one's will and heart. This situation entails the risk of succumbing to inanity and also that of an interior breakdown or a personality imbalance. This danger sometimes pushes us to great lengths and even so far as violence, crime and certain other antisocial behavior, the various forms of which are frequently studied and discussed.

Another phenomenon of this type often seen in today's generation is that of rebellion. Rebellion and protest are different from frustration. Rebellion even contains a positive element, so long as it is a struggle for authentic values and not simply unmotivated and self-centered revolt.

If rebellion entails the search for authentic values, it is possible to encounter Christ in it. Such rebellion sometimes grows within us because of a feeling that life is hopeless, aimless and superficial. People often discuss this and try to provide some explanation for the sickness and suggest some treatment.

It is suggested that rebelliousness, and also the feeling of the hopelessness of life, can be lessened or relieved through work. Now I must tell you that this "work ethic" is not a satisfactory prescription. However it is taken, work cannot satisfy the person or fulfill the deepest needs of his humanity. Unless it is taken as the fulfillment of service and love, it can neither satisfy the person, nor give release from the feeling of rebelliousness, nor provide reassurance in the face of even the slightest frustration.

However, work can contribute toward the accomplishment of service and love, and we should therefore be careful not to view it in purely utilitarian terms or solely from the perspective of the material advantage or profit it appears to involve. We should be careful about this for our own good and be sure to avoid this concept of work, and also this view of life, because they can make us stray far from our course toward what we believe are our objectives. Means alone cannot solve human problems. We are destined toward a specific end, and we should therefore be careful to avoid a solely utilitarian conception of work.

If work and means which, taken in a material sense, should make us rich are taken as ends in themselves, we shall remain poor. This is closely linked to our conception of work and our way of viewing it. If work is not seen as an expression of service and love and is empty of human value, it can destroy the person. However, work can also possess those values which promote human growth. We can feel and see it not as something extraneous to us, coming to us from outside, but rather as something of our own, something within us, which we create.

The beneficiary of our work constitutes another aspect, and this is where, to a large extent, we find the possibility of seeing work as service and love. There is no work which cannot bring us closer to God and our fellow human beings. There are types of work which have people as their immediate beneficiaries (for example, the work of a doctor, nurse, teacher, or priest), whereas others are only indirectly concerned with them (for example the work of an engineer or builder). Other people are involved wherever and whatever my work may be; if we take the installation of a furnace, the construction of a spiral stairway or the painting of a house as examples, each of these jobs is, in the final analysis, useful in some way. It is useful to other people and can therefore take its place in the order of service and love.

If I bear in mind the beneficiary of my work and see it in terms of service and love, it forms an important element of Christianity; it is a very important aspect of our being with Christ, which is something we talked about yesterday. This element is not mentioned in any labor statistics, and still less in any labor codes. It must be elaborated within ourselves, since it springs from our interiority and our attitude of commitment. It is present from the very first steps, when we are still poring over schoolbooks or absorbing whole columns of figures; if we take figures as an example, they will

lead us back to the furnace or the spiral stairway, and hence
to the person.

I also want to talk to you about the second outstanding
and fundamental positive aspect in Christ's human life, and
one which is often found in the individual's life.

This second positive aspect is suffering. This statement
may startle you. It startles me, too, every time I am at the
bedside of suffering person who has reached the limits of
endurance and pain.

This afternoon I heard someone say something with
which I am in full agreement: "Only somebody who has ex-
perienced something really knows it. Before that, you have
a concept of it rather like a blind man's concept of color."
Nobody knows about pain like those who suffer. However,
it is a fact that very often the suffering of others has an edi-
fying effect for us. I myself did not believe this was possible, but now I have often seen it and this is why I say that
suffering is a positive element, even though it may be very
problematic. Further, this positive element is derived from
Christ's position, and from our position with Christ.

We look at suffering only from without, whereas we
should be looking at it from within. Apart from its exterior
aspect, suffering also has an interior aspect, and this is a
mystery which unfolds within people.

I remember visiting someone who was once a student
here. He is older than you and is now unable to move from
his sickbed and has no hope of doing so. Even so, when you
enter his room he has a smile on his face, and it is not a
forced smile but a true, radiant one. This is incomprehensible if you consider only the exterior aspect of this man,
whose body is so ravaged that he can no longer turn the
pages of a book with his own hand. His radiance is an inde-
cipherable mystery when looked at from an exterior viewpoint.

When we meet with suffering we meet with Christ, and this is why it is a positive element in life.

Now let us return a moment to the first essential and fundamental positive element found in Christ's human life and in the human life of each person: love. Here I am thinking of family love.

Institution is an overly weak and formalistic term to describe the family. Other expressions like *household, society* or *community* are none of them correct; the family is more an *environment* or *home*. It is an environment in which people are formed by mutual exchange, not only in the relationship of parents with their children but also in that of children with their parents. Parents are good teachers if they too are able to learn. This is a very positive aspect of the family, a fundamental positive aspect of human life.

Today we are witnessing a certain crisis. It is difficult to analyze the crisis at this point, but one of its symptoms is that young people do not admire the family and their own parents but are looking for another model. Sometimes—indeed, often—they also rebel.

Maybe the war is to blame. Maybe this disintegration of the family is linked to that cataclysm which upset everything human and all human values, or maybe it is a deeper, interior crisis. Be that as it may, the crisis does exist and it is accompanied by a certain anxiety which often seems to go very deep indeed, so that very often we do not know where this thirst for seeking will lead us, or even if it is truly a search and not simply a negation.

I would beg my young listeners to reflect seriously as to whether they are seeking or simply negating.

We also have the fourth commandment, which says: "Honor your father and your mother, that your days may be long" (Exodus 20:12). We often recite this commandment, but I do not know whether we understand it fully, since none of the other commandments is formulated in the same way. Most of the Ten Commandments are in the form of prohibitions—"You shall not kill. You shall not commit adultery. You shall not steal," and so on—whereas here we are simply told to "honor." There is also the final phrase, " . . . that your days may be long." The Israelites most probably interpreted this longevity primarily in a literal sense, but there is another deeper meaning to these words.

To honor them means to respect their value as persons. Being human means learning from others, from our parents. At this point some of you may be wondering bitterly, "How *could* I have learned? How *could* I have learned if my father abandoned my mother? Or if this man who happens to be called the husband of my mother isn't my real father? Or if this woman who happens to be called the wife of my father isn't my real mother? Honor!" But, yes, this is what God expects. I know it can sometimes seem a great deal.

Let us see how the crisis can come about and also the tremendous responsibility it entails—responsibility toward the most fundamental human values: " . . . that your days may be long." Must this necessarily be taken in a literal sense and as referring to material prosperity, or is it maybe not more important that a deep sense of human value and dignity should come from the family? Then, even if one lives for only a short time, one's life is long. One's life is not long if one has not discovered that which is of greater value than created things.

My dear children, we must reflect seriously on the fourth commandment so that the crisis in the family and the resulting crisis in parent-child relationships may not be too harsh in their effects. We must study it in depth in order to make sure that what we can produce will be better or at least equally good. Have we become so caught up in the processes of this crisis that we tend to think of it as something normal? And can we be sure that our own model, which we carry in the depths of our consciousness, is better than the other one?

One can sometimes hear the most incredible ideas expressed, for example: "There should be joint 'marriages,' because one-to-one unions are pure selfishness, with other people excluded from a relationship in which the partners want to keep themselves solely for one another."

My dear children, how can we test, verify and control our ideas, since they can lead us into very strange paths in which we may even sometimes lose sight of where they are leading? We move forward blindly, even though these matters entail great responsibility. Even so, it must be admitted that on the whole young people do take these matters seriously—as we can see from recent events, discussions and publications.

My dear children, the only way for us to examine and solve these problems is the way Christ developed and solved them. What he said in this regard can be applied to and benefit everybody; he asked something not only *of* the person, but also *for* the person. "What God has joined together, let no man put asunder" (Matthew 19:6). This is *for* the person. And everything Christ said in this context has the precise purpose of serving us and not that of placing a burden on us, since its aim is to guarantee dignity and love for the person.

Christ said, "You shall not commit adultery," repeating what we find in the Old Testament. When he added that "Every one who looks at a woman lustfully has already committed adultery with her in his heart" (Matthew 5:28), he was not asking for something which goes against the human race and is beyond human capacity.

This must be seen as one of the most important positive elements in Christ's position. The human person and this "positive humanity" constitute important—and, indeed, fundamental—values. My personhood, and the personhood of each individual. My personhood, and what I have which is of positive value. "What will it profit a man, if he gains the whole world and forfeits his life?" (Matthew 16:28). How true this is! When we talk about the soul, we are talking about personhood, which the Lord Jesus set above all other things.

This is the greatest positive thing I have. It is mine. Any automobile, television set, or machine, is a means and is extrinsic to me. But this is what I am! And I must look after this great positive aspect and develop it with care.

The question of responsibility springs from this.

Amen

4. A Talk for Female Students

There are many things of common interest to all of us, but here I want to address myself exclusively to you women.

When we study the Gospel carefully we can see that Christ assigns women a special place beside him and offers them different possibilities from those open to men. This is why I have decided to devote the second part of today's talk specifically to you. Similarly, I shall dedicate the second part of tomorrow's time to the men.

We shall focus our attention on the specific role entrusted to women by Christ.

I would ask you to bring to mind all Christ's meetings with women, and theirs with him—and we find many cases of both in the Gospel—so that we can arrive at a balanced and integrated interpretation. There were such episodes as his conversation with the woman of Samaria, his meeting with Mary Magdalene, and that with Lazarus' two sisters, Martha and Mary, and also the person of Mary, his own mother. We find a wide variety of personalities, and can observe their relationships with Christ in a number of different situations.

The first thing which strikes us is that when they approached Christ these women acquired a certain interior autonomy, even those who were "fallen women." One clear example of this is the woman of Samaria, whose conversation with Christ is reported in the fourth chapter of Saint John's Gospel. This meeting with the woman of Samaria takes on the character of a real "event"! Do you remember their conversation beside the well? Christ asked for water, and the woman was surprised that he, as a Jew, would ask water from her, a Samaritan. The conversation then moved on from natural to supernatural water, the water of life, which is the drink of the immortal soul. At a certain point Christ told her: "Go, call your husband, and come here." "I have no husband," she answered. "You are right in saying, 'I have no husband'; for you have had five husbands and he whom you now have is not your husband." We find a sort of liberation in the woman's reaction: Christ has set her free by revealing the truth. He has gained her trust and shown her the significance of her position. There must have been something in this conversation which did not humiliate or mortify her, crushing her, but relieved her.

The same thing happened with Mary Magdalene.

Let us also recall Christ's words to Martha and Mary in the village of Bethany. He spoke to Martha in a most surprising way: "You are anxious and troubled about many things; only one thing is needed" (Luke 10:41–42). It seems that he wanted to reprove Martha, the worker, who was too taken up with her tasks and gave no thought to her interior life, so that she was not free.

In every Gospel episode involving meetings with women, they find their independence at Christ's side. This feature is particularly striking in the case of the Mother of Christ. Mary is a very simple person, but has great individuality and is very much herself. Her motherhood itself was the fruit of choice: "Let it be to me according to your word" (Luke 1:38). This phrase decided everything, then and for the future. We have very few details about the Holy Mother, but those few details we do find in the Gospel tell us a great deal and enable us to see her individuality as a woman.

She was not only Christ's Mother, but also a mature, independent companion throughout his life. We see this in the Gospel, from the marriage feast of Cana to Calvary.

With Christ there are no slaves, even if the social system at that time treated women as slaves, not only in Rome but also among the Jews. There are no slaves at Christ's side. The public sinner becomes a promised bride, a sister. However, a woman is above all a mother.

Let us consider the whole question of the concept of emancipation. Old as this concept may be, we are today witnessing its spread, so that it has had an equalizing effect between men and women in various ways, in both professional and political fields and in our very lifestyle.

Equality between men and women is completely comprehensible, so long as it is based exclusively on the inner maturity and independence of women, as we find these illustrated in the Gospel. Without a sense of being an individual and of planning her own life and future, exterior emancipation will destroy a woman instead of improving her position. There is no doubt that this exterior emancipation and equality with men often produce split personalities in women, especially those with professional training. The tasks, duties and problems of their lives simply double, and conflicts are generated.

Let us consider a woman's interior character as compared with that of a man. Christ understood this difference perfectly. Women are more feeling and intuitive people and become involved in things in a more sensitive and complete manner. This is why they need a support (for example, in the Gospel we find them "by Christ's side"), great maturity and interior independence.

It may sound paradoxical, but this independence simultaneously makes the woman free of love and open to it. It

makes her free of love with a small *l*—love as necessity, re-
striction, mere occasion, or eroticism—and opens her to the
Love which is the fruit of conscious choice and in which she
can find her own life and vocation. However paradoxical it
may be, this need is inescapable, since women take part
with the whole of their sensitivity.

They are much more susceptible than men to things like
psychological conditioning and must therefore gain this independence through an interior struggle which does not
banish love from their lives but instead recognizes it as the
underlying motivation in the Great Love of which they are
capable.

This autonomy is also necessary from a social viewpoint.
With Christ women are independent, and, so to speak, do
not need men; when they get married, this independence
means that they are persons and not objects.

Here is where there can be so much disappointment or
delusion. Without the mediation of love, a woman remains
an object for a man. I am thinking of remarks like this: "I
married very young, without finishing school, and now I
am suffering enormously." The story continues, and we can
summarize the reasons for her suffering as follows: "I suffer
because I'm an object and not a person." "Doesn't your
husband show any sensitivity and sympathy towards you?"
"No. He always wants just one thing." This is even more
painful if it is the conclusion of what you thought was love
and to which you gave yourself wholeheartedly.

This is why a woman needs interior emancipation, which
means that, in love, she can stand beside the man as companion and together they can build something. This is a
woman's basic vocation and it explains the nature of marriage. Marriage is not simply an institutionalization of the
sexual life. If this were the case it would destroy any feelings of the two partners, and especially those of the woman.

This is why a woman is first and foremost a mother. A mother is the person who generates, which means bringing up—and bringing up not only children—with love and intuition. Her basic task is that of educating, and when she shares the responsibility for it with men she cannot be simply an object for them. It is noteworthy that Jesus Christ, the Son of God, God made man, allowed himself to be educated by a woman, his mother; this is significant for us.

With Christ women blossom as mothers. When a woman is, so to speak, defined by her beauty and her feelings, one sometimes has the impression that she fits comfortably into the role of an object—the object of admiration, the center of attraction, a doll, and finally something that is simply "used."

Women must develop what I would call a spiritual instinct for self-preservation, and a certain method of defending their own personalities. The path to this is interior independence. Women must also bring men to recognize their independence and to see that this female independence in no way threatens their union, but on the contrary helps form and strengthen it. The man must come to understand that the woman is a person, that she can be a mother, and that motherhood is a wonderful thing and a profound experience—and one in which the man cannot simply assume the role of spectator. With her motherhood she communicates to him the inestimable value of fatherhood.

You may be thinking that he receives this without giving anything in exchange, while she pays for it! However, the fact that she pays means that she must certainly take her motherhood seriously. It is a terrible insult when people ask us, "Well, what do you want?" These people are for the most part Catholic women; and they destroy unborn babies. "What do you want?" We have a great responsibility and duty to fulfill.

You can reasonably ask me: "Why are you saying all this to *us*? You priests always talk to us, but what about the men?" Rest assured, I shall speak to them; I shall speak to them man to man, from this same pulpit. But I am speaking to you now, because it is also in your own interests.

Men must learn that motherhood not only ennobles, but that it is a dreadful thing when it is destroyed at conception, together with the child who is the fruit of this maternity. This is a terrible tragedy, and it cannot be permitted to continue; nor can it be ignored. It is a danger which is around us every day.

For many of you this problem may seem to concern the future, and a distant future, at that. However, it must not take you unawares. It is really a very difficult matter and is fraught with problems. Men must be taught to love, and to love in a noble way; they must be educated in depth in this truth, that is, in the fact that a woman is a person and not simply an object. With this objective in mind, this question must therefore be discussed in depth and in time, while we are still concerned with our university lectures, or maybe even while we are studying our high school books. In depth and in time.

We hear a number of different opinions and suggested solutions regarding this question, but they are only apparent solutions, because they do not take the person into account. The human person is missing. One thing Christ does require is that the human person should not be omitted in any solution.

These tasks are extremely difficult. I do not want to depress or frighten you, but simply to let you know that we realize how fraught with problems your task is. I also want to add that we have no intention of simply being moralizers who spend their time correcting you, since we are aware of the sacrifices and difficulties of life today. We are familiar

with the painful background to these phenomena. And
Christ understood even better. As he still does today!

Can I tell you what to do? I have already done so in part.
You should ask other people—for instance, your mother—
for further advice; but be sure you ask people who will tell
you the truth and will not minimize the task, because there
are certain opinions in this regard (and they are often found
even within Christian families) which are not at all Christian.

Another thing: if you asked me precisely what you
should do and where you should seek advice in this regard,
I would maybe not be able to give you a very detailed answer. However, I do know for sure that with Christ all
women—each and every one of them—possess maturity
and interior independence, which are the most important
factors. They are what are essential for forming and developing personality, training for motherhood, and growth in
love and responsibility. So the only thing I can tell you is
that you should draw closer and closer to Christ, and not
just superficially as a passing frame of mind, but with your
whole heart, your whole being and your whole life. Seek
him and draw closer to him.

You know how to do this. You have known since you
were small children, and I do not need to teach you how to
approach Christ. I simply want to assure you that with him
each and every woman gains her interior independence.

Yesterday we said that choosing God means choosing
oneself, one's own self. Choosing Christ means choosing
oneself. So how better could you choose yourselves anew,
with your female, feminine individuality and your own selfhood, than with Christ? This is all that is involved. And
how are you to do this? You will certainly be guided in this
understanding by the interior light and the grace which always helps us, the "grace of state." If you seek you will
find.

In any case, in the path of love which life entails, always remember that above every love there is one Love. One Love. Love without constraint or hesitation. It is the love with which Christ loves each one of you.

Amen

5. Sin

The content of the Gospels is deeply human, since it is the truth about man's life, and this is precisely why it also contains the negative aspect. The picture presented in the Gospels is real and true.

Refusal is the essence of the negative aspects of which I am speaking. It is obviously the opposite of the attitude of service and love incarnated by Christ himself.

There are a number of these negative elements found around Christ in the Gospels. The negative element is sin, and, since the Gospel is not a description of utopia or some idyllic event, but is rich in human content, there are quite a number of sins around Christ in the Gospels. Christ, the Son of God, became man in order to redeem us from sin, and consequently sin had to be found around Christ in the Gospels.

The Gospels are thus grafted into every human life, and every human life is in various ways grafted into the Gospels. We can therefore find the basis of our human life in them, and this is the reason for their universal relevance, their universality: they concern each individual person. This is why they are always contemporary and relevant and never go out of fashion.

Each period of history is full of negative aspects of sin, and our contemporary world has its full share. We must face up to the fact that there are many of these in us and around us.

Let us imagine some ordinary human situation we could meet with any day in our office, home or laboratory. One or more of these places may be dominated by an unpleasant atmosphere, an atmosphere of animosity, or at least insensitivity, an atmosphere which contaminates and in some way affects everything and everyone; and this atmosphere may exclude or emarginate some people. Today we often hear talk about broken or emarginated people.

Where does this atmosphere come from? It comes from us, from somebody who gives it form—maybe one or two of us, or maybe all of us. We probably all contribute to it, some of us actively and others passively, some of us through commission and others through omission. It is a very common situation.

At home doors are slammed, and the different members of the family do not speak to one another, and live their lives closed off from one another, as if they were total strangers and there were a wall between them. This too is a common situation.

We must admit that in these situations it is often more a case of general human suffering and dissatisfaction and of hidden tears than of some consciously and freely willed evil.

The catechism definition of sin says that it is evil which is consciously and freely willed. Even so, evil is brought about almost unconsciously and unfreely, almost against our own will. It is difficult to say that this happens completely separately from and independently of us. Evil has its source somewhere. It springs from the will of a person who is not able—or, rather, willing—to prevent it.

Is evil solely a question of will, of what I want or do not want, or is it sometimes a question of ignorance? Again, is such ignorance simply a lack of knowledge or is it also a certain lack of commitment? These difficulties could be overcome if we made an effort, but we do not try, so that these various omissions or shortcomings weave a constant pattern through our lives; thus, we have what can be called ill will, or a lack of good will, in us.

Some situations of this type are particularly clear, and I should like to give an example of this. A woman gives birth to a baby, which she and her husband have both been looking forward to, so that it should be a moment of joy. However, two weeks later, the husband meets another woman. He tells this second woman that he loves her and that he wants to leave his wife and child. He starts lying and rationalizing, trying to find some excuse and to attribute the guilt elsewhere, since clearly he is not the guilty party! And the other woman does all she can to keep him. In this case it is fairly easy to recognize the source of the evil. If the husband or the mistress would admit that the evil comes from them, everything would be simple. The problem lies in the fact that neither of them is willing to assume responsibility for this evil.

Sometimes the question of sin can seem so simple! When we first learn in our catechism classes what sin is, even the very sound of the word arouses our disapproval. How simple everything was then! But then we manage to complicate matters and falsify even simple things. This is why the problem of sin is in fact a problem and the truth about sin is such a hard truth. It is a hard truth to accept, not in a generalized or abstract way, not in some novel or play, and not when it concerns others: it is hard to accept within myself.

Further, we usually think that sin is a question of a specific moment or action, whereas this is not the case. There is always a certain process leading up to it. Sin never occurs as something sudden and unexpected; it develops bit by bit. It may appear that it develops without our being aware of it; however, this is only an impression. It is not an unexpected thing, which takes us by surprise. The groundwork for it is laid in a certain way from outside—and, we must point out, from inside too.

It is generally thought and claimed that circumstances produce it from outside, but this is not the case! Sin does not come from without; we do not commit it through some anonymous impulse or force, since this would eliminate personal choice from the picture. It is a very specific and definite force which begins in a person, in one of us . . . in me! Let us look at it in this perspective.

Sin is a certain type of process. First of all it is for a long time something of its own, before becoming actual sin. And then there is a certain "post-sin" process.

The pre-sin process is called temptation. "I have given in to temptation; I yielded to temptation," we say. Temptation acts from outside; but it also acts from within me. And it has its own allies. The first allies of temptation are a certain superficiality and frivolity. Yes, frivolity, inasmuch as we do not take moral problems seriously. We do not think that sin can take place in and through ourselves. Another way of looking at this is as lack of trust in God. This is how sin matures: lack of trust in God is just the right atmosphere for the development of temptation!

Then, suddenly, at a certain moment—maybe the most unexpected moment—a limit is reached. Certain moral reserves, such as prudence and modesty, and other things which each of us is familiar with, have come to an end. Undoubtedly, those reserves which represent a certain interior resistance to evil have run out.

Now the post-sin process sets in. This process would appear to leave a sort of path for a return to the pre-sin situation. However, this seldom takes place. What very often happens is that sin makes claims on us, urging us on to further sin. Sin breeds sin. There are certain sins which do not lead further, but there are others which do.

The person suddenly finds himself under the power of a force which he himself has set in motion. This is how habitual sin and a number of bad habits are formed within us. And in time, my dear children, these become stupid sins. Yes, stupid sins! Let us take habitual drunkenness as an example. It is horrifying, but it is a stupid sin. And it is stupid not because it makes us act stupidly, but because the pleasure gained is truly nothing when set against what we lose, so that it can only be described as stupidity. Even so, this sin really does destroy people. It destroys people, however capable they may be, when they begin to go beyond the limits of choice, at the least expected moment. And then it entangles and entraps them and they do not have the option of turning back: they are no longer able to turn back! But this is not true: it is always possible to turn back!

Sin is obviously something personal, something of one's own. However, there are also the sins of others. When we reflect on our lives we often overlook the fact that there are sins of other people for which we have at least been the cause—the cause of moral evil.

There are of course sins of different types, some large and some small. The catechism refers to venial and mortal sins, that is, light and serious ones.

The measure of the seriousness of a sin is always related to the individual, and this is explained very clearly by C.S. Lewis, who writes that for a person who has hereditary defects and who has received a defective moral education, any sins will be small, because of his particular objective condition, whereas for another person, who is differently disposed and has a different conscience, the same sins will be serious.

The measure of a sin is always individual, and this is why

we cannot evaluate the sins of another person, even if certain norms do exist. Only God can measure the sin of each of us, and this is why the problem of good and evil cannot be based anywhere but in God.

This does not mean that it is not formed within us in accord with the perspective of our own conscience. People often emphasize the link between the conscience and God, calling it the voice of God. This may be a metaphor, but it is quite an effective one, inasmuch as the measure of good and evil is linked to the conscience. In our conscience anything can be true or false. Consciences can err. There are scrupulous consciences which exaggerate evil and see it everywhere, and there are lax ones which really do not bother even about serious evil.

A healthy conscience, which can judge the moral value of our actions correctly, is an immense treasure! We must work constantly towards the formation of this type of conscience. However, it should be not only healthy, but also delicate and sensitive, because sometimes a healthy conscience may be rather rough and unrefined, so that it examines each situation separately, evaluating it carefully, but without relating it to deeper matters and without discerning those things which probably involve us from a moral viewpoint. One must work carefully on one's own conscience, since it is such a delicate instrument that if it is not continually tuned it can lose its tone or go completely out of tune.

We must put in a great deal of work on our own conscience. If you ask me whose interest this is in and who will benefit from it, the answer is that it is in our own interest and that we shall ourselves benefit. Each of us is responsible for the formation of his or her own conscience. Our humanity is expressed in being moral; it is expressed in and through the conscience; and this is why we must forge our conscience.

Maybe you will say: "All right, I'll work away at my conscience, so it becomes healthy and sensitive, even though
people around me have lax, unrefined consciences." And
you may add that these are the very people who appear to
thrive and prosper. This is of course so from one viewpoint;
however, it does not take into consideration the value of humanity itself, which is in fact the most essential aspect. Although it is sometimes very difficult for us to struggle
against this way of looking at things, we must make the effort, since the battle which each person—and particularly
each Christian—fights for humanity and human values is
the noblest of battles. It is a frontline battle, and final victory is worth the risk of some losses.

Another point is that sin constitutes conflict with God.
People worry about this matter a great deal, wondering
where this conflict with God springs from and whether it is
found in every sin.

Let us return a moment to the day before yesterday's
talk, when we said that the person chooses or refuses God.
We choose God when we choose ourselves, and we are constantly choosing or refusing God. In each action when we
choose ourselves we are choosing (or refusing) God—this is
how closely we are linked to God!

So why does sin always give rise to conflict with God? I
would say that it is because sin is against the "ideology" of
God. God's ideology is that of creation, and it lies in creating and in developing the good, particularly in the moral order. Sin, on the other hand, destroys. In the first place it destroys the fundamental good with which we are all imbued.
Sin destroys the good which is the person, the good which
is myself.

I did not give myself existence, and I do not own myself.
In the final analysis, not even my parents gave me existence. God has a fundamental right over us, since he cre-

ated us. As his creatures we are in a certain manner pervaded by the ideology of God who creates and through whom all growth takes place. And if I wreak ruin and destruction around and within myself, this is in ideological conflict with God: I am professing some ideology other than his.

Apart from this, it is also naturally a conflict of wills, inasmuch as thought acts through the intellect and the intellect goes hand in hand with the will. Thanks to my intellect, I recognize the moral norms and principles according to which I should do one thing and avoid another. In his self-revelation God has defined and highlighted these norms and principles. "You shall have no other gods besides me; honor your father and your mother; you shall not kill," and so on. In view of this, I know what his will is, so that it is not simply a conflict of ideas but also a conflict between his will and mine, in which I want something different from what he wants.

One last question, and an even deeper one. Why is sin conflict with Christ?

Nietzsche wrote a philosophical work entitled *Beyond Good and Evil*. Human beings do have a desire to place themselves beyond good and evil, in an effort to achieve personal freedom beyond morality, liberating themselves from what is most human—in other words, morality. However, Christ rejected such an idea, placing himself in the center, between good and evil, and taking a personal part in the conflict between good and evil as it is found in every human being. By doing so, he made it the duty of each of us to do the same. Therefore, any person who tries to place himself beyond good and evil, beyond morality, is not with Christ.

We have already said that the Christian is a person whose place is beside Christ; this person therefore takes on the whole burden of morality—for morality *is* a burden, as well as being an instrument of elevation. The person who wants to be with Christ must take on his shoulders the whole burden of morality, which will be the instrument of his elevation. If we refuse this burden, we are in conflict with Christ.

We try to thrust the cross away from us, because morality is cross; and everything that has been written about the cross in numerous studies, novels and plays cannot be compared with the single concept of morality as cross. Christian morality, and morality in general, means the cross. We may even try to thrust the cross away from us; but Christ did not thrust it from his shoulders; and therefore sin is conflict with Christ.

We are slowly coming to the end of our retreat, and I want to devote tomorrow to prayer. The Blessed Sacrament will be exposed in this church throughout the day, and I warmly urge you to come and spent time in adoration.

And now I want to talk specifically to the men among you.

6. A Talk for Male Students

In Saint Matthew's Gospel (19:16–22) we read about Christ's conversation with the rich young man. I shall just remind you of the more salient points.

The young man comes to Jesus and asks him: "Teacher, what good deed must I do, to have eternal life?" Jesus answers: "If you would enter life, keep the commandments." The young man asks another question, "Which?", and Jesus reminds him of the Ten Commandments. The young man's reaction is: "All these I have observed; what do I still lack?" Then Jesus says: "If you would be perfect, go, sell what you possess and give to the poor . . . and come, follow me." And then we have the reaction of the young man: without a single word, he turns and leaves.

Let us try to examine this episode from the human viewpoint, whereas it is more often analyzed from various other viewpoints.

In a human perspective we can explain it as follows. The young man is in some way drawn to what Jesus is saying. He understands that he is proclaiming some sort of good— a good which he too would like to achieve and which is called the Kingdom of God. So what must he do? What specific thing? The young man's question sounds positive. Even so, we cannot see his response to Jesus' advice in a positive light.

Let us look at the episode as a whole. When Jesus tells

him to observe the commandments, and then lists them, the young man answers that he has observed them all from an early age. A general picture of this man begins to emerge. We could see him as an honest, sensible and upright person. However, we could also see him rather differently. At this point the young man feels that he is in a sense superior to Jesus. "What are you proclaiming?" "What do you want?" "This isn't beyond my capabilities, or different from my present life. So, in a certain sense, you are not superior to me; I am on the same level as you, or maybe on a higher one." We do not find this in the Gospel text. However, this further psychological aspect can be read between the lines of the text.

We all have a certain male arrogance. This young man had his share of this arrogance, and his reaction was in line with it.

If we take this factor into account, then the remainder of the conversation makes sense and its lesson becomes clear to us.

Jesus asks him a question or, rather, issues a challenge: "If you would be perfect, go, sell what you possess and give to the poor, . . . and come, follow me." "Follow me." This is an offer and a challenge. He is no longer talking about things the young man can do with relatively little effort, since he has already answered that "All these I have observed from my youth." Instead, Jesus is asking him to give. And here we gain a glimpse of another male characteristic: our lack of willingness to give.

We are quite ready to take, or conquer, in terms of enjoyment, profit, gain and success—and even in the moral order. Then comes the question of giving, and at this point we hang back, because we are not prepared to give. The element which is so characteristic under other forms in the spiritual portrait of women is barely perceptible in men.

Our analysis of this Gospel incident can now be used as the starting point for our specific reflection on your particular condition in life, because it is easy to discern similar traits and elements in the spiritual portrait of each of us: male arrogance, scant willingness to give, and the spirit of conquest.

We have a spirit of conquest and domination in the various spheres of life, and this can also be our attitude in religious matters.

There is a certain tendency to see religion as a women's matter and something rather unsuitable for men. Men always feel more at home in the role of Nicodemus. Do you remember? Nicodemus was the member of the Sanhedrin who recognized Jesus, but only in secret. I am not saying that he already believed in him; however, he recognized him and visited him by night, at times when nobody would see him. We have a tendency toward the Nicodemus type of religious attitude, toward the type of devotion which is characterized maybe only by superficial discretion but very often also by fear of what others might think.

We are reluctant to commit ourselves. We are just like that young man, who was very willing to take everything he could from Christ, in a spirit of conquest, but who went away when it came to committing himself.

However, it can also be a simple question of circumstances, since it is only fair to admit, for example, that, quite apart from your presence here today and the general presence of men in our churches today, our Polish Catholicism is becoming more and more masculine and less feminine. I feel that in today's age of tension and conflict, the problems of faith and religion do to some extent call forth this type of testimony.

However, even though more men go to church, so that sometimes they even outnumber the women, and even though we can therefore claim that our Catholicism is becoming more masculine and less feminine, the picture is not quite the same as regards deep commitment. This male Catholicism is not interior and deep enough; the male believer does not have a true interior life. What he maybe thinks of as his own particular religious style—this discretion and distance or detachment from devotional practices and the sacramental life—in effect means that his interior life is defective and lacking in depth. Even looked at from another perspective, this is really the result of the fact that we men do not have a deep enough interior life. Our Catholicism may therefore be more masculine, but it is not deep enough.

Moreover, we cannot leave the affairs of the Kingdom of God to women, and the reason for this is that Christ gave clear instructions in this regard when he told his Apostles: "Go therefore and make disciples of all nations" (Matthew 28:19). This means, "Go and teach," which in turn means that we must take responsibility for the Gospel as Truth! In contemporary terms it means that, in accordance with our specific characteristics as men, we must take responsibility for the Gospel as *Weltanschauung* and idea. In men the intellect has a certain supremacy over the heart, and this is why Christ entrusted responsibility for the Gospel as idea to them. The Gospel is life and we are all responsible for it. Women have a great role to play in the Church, and in Catholicism; however, the Gospel as idea is primarily a male sphere.

Christ said that we should go out and teach. My dear sons, this does not refer only to bishops and priests, but to all of us. Now, when have you, as grown men, taught somebody? Have you taught any children their catechism? Or started a discussion of some religious topic with a colleague? You may feel that such matters are embarrassing, but here we must make a clear distinction between discretion and cowardice or simple superficiality. You probably do not discuss religious matters or even think about them at all. Oh, how superficial you are! But Christ said: "Go out and teach." When you are a father (as some of you already may be): "Go and teach." When you kneel with your child in prayer: "Teach!"

You will maybe object, as people used to, that this is not your problem, but that it is a matter for women and that women must teach children to say their prayers. Maybe this is true of the words of the prayers, but surely it does not apply to the teaching of prayer itself or of a religious sense? "Go and teach."

My dear sons, we should remember that we men have a special responsibility with regard to spreading the concept of the Gospel. Responsibility for the Gospel has been left far too much to women, and we must make sure that those who are growing up now recognize this. Husbands usually tell their wives that it is completely up to them to deal with these matters. But Christ said, "Go and teach," and he was saying this to you! This instruction should be taken in its broader sense; the method of teaching is one thing, and the duty to teach another.

As I have already noted, when we examine Christ's meeting with the rich young man and consider the psychological dialogue between the lines, we can see the young man's male arrogance and his lack of willingness to give of himself. However, we can also see a certain tendency to impose his own human interpretation on what is God's truth or will. This is obviously a general human tendency, but it applies in a particular way to men.

I feel that I must make God's truth and will fit into my perspective, and my concern is whether or not they are convenient for me. For *me*! If it is convenient or helpful to me, well and good, but if not, I refuse it and leave. There is the temptation to place myself "above" Christ, especially when he asks something of me.

Maybe this temptation to follow our own inclinations and wishes to place ourselves "beyond" Christ is found particularly in the field of sexual morality, because it is here that Christ makes demands on men. These demands are greater than we think, but they are not made in the way we imagine; his demands are made differently from the way we normally make them.

What usually happens in the case of a man is that he is the one whose desire is strongest and it is he who urges his partner on, and who "takes." On the other hand, it is the woman who pays, while very often the man is unwilling to pay anything at all. Often when the woman has to pay personally, all he says is: "Go and find a doctor. I'll give you the money." While she pays personally, he pays with money! Or he may try to shift the blame, saying: "It's your fault. Why did you let this happen? It's your fault, not mine." But it is he whose desire was so overwhelming and who "took"!

However, the point is this: when he takes his pleasure he must also take his responsibility.

My dear sons, these rather crude expressions I have just given as examples are not particularly unusual.

Maybe what I am about to tell you will seem premature. However, you should be prepared for the future and begin to assume gradual responsibility for it.

We are dealing here with a twofold question, the first aspect being that of you and the Creator, and the second that of you and your partner.

First, let us consider the aspect of you and the Creator. My dear brothers, God, who is Father, is first of all Creator, and this God who is Father, who is Creator, planted a reflection of his creative strength and power within man. We can approach creation biologically, so that the whole matter is viewed in natural terms. However, it has its inner significance in God. Since biology and nature come from God, the seeds of life which each of us carried within his body are the basis of our participation in God's creative force. God creates, which means that he calls something into existence from nothing. And man creates inasmuch as he gives life. This is why each of us must have deep respect for the essence and nature of things. We should sing hymns of praise to God the Creator for this reflection of himself in us—and not only in our souls but also in our bodies.

Now, let us consider the aspect of you and your partner. Although it is true that man is the creator of life, this life is created within the woman. It is another law of nature that they create this life together; they unite more closely in order to bring this life into being. However, this is a very special moment and is particularly important because the man is the creator of life within her; but it is she who takes on the whole burden of this life immediately afterwards. And, precisely because of this factor, this is where a frightening moral danger begins, since the man can fall into the role of a primitive profiteer or exploiter. He will in fact always do so, if he does not make use of his own interior strength—the strength of his intellect and his will and even his heart—in order to mature in the role of father.

God is Creator and Father.

It is precisely when a man does not mature into the role of father that we hear him say things like: "Go and find a doctor. I'll give you the money. Why on earth did you let this happen? There is such a thing as contraception." However, she has a right to your recognition of your paternity and to your assumption of responsibility and your protection.

We make very little effort to understand how women think and feel, so that resentment sets in and wounds are opened in the soul; a woman feels walls of isolation, incomprehension and destruction springing up between her and the man who was so close to her. And our arrogance and pride prevent us from seeing all this; our attitude is that of a conqueror or captor.

We should like this difficult problem to solve itself. However, it will not go away on its own; it is you who must solve it. Not her, but first and foremost you. Men have a certain tendency to leave this problem up to the woman: "You should have known. You really should have known." If she should have known, you should have known too! You must accept responsibility for this person who will be born.

This is not only a demographic or economic problem, but a deep moral one. My dear brothers, I beg you not to forget that this is a moral problem. Why do we try to believe that this is not so? You are no longer sixteen years old, and we must face this question and solve it. I say *we* since this applies to us priests too, because in the course of conversations through the grille of the confessional we are sometimes left speechless when faced with the absolute authority of this new existence. So this matter involves us too.

Of course, from both the economic and demographic viewpoints some solution is required for the population question. The Church is seeking a solution, and has asked doctors and other specialists throughout the world to carry out research in this field.

Such solutions are often rather abstract, since the real solution must be given by each one of us, and it certainly does not lie only in natural birth control (although natural family planning does represent a great step forward) but also in the development of a correct attitude toward love. The expression and demonstration of love does not always mean that conception must take place. We should give careful consideration to this question and not forget it.

Our retreat brings us face to face with Christ, and we come to understand the general line of his teachings, as reflected on in our meditations. My dear sons, in the Gospel we see many different men in a number of different relationships with Jesus. It is a sort of composite picture of humanity, with figures representing each one of us even today.

We find Pilate, who has a discussion with Jesus and at one point seems close to him, but all this leads simply to a general question, "What is the truth?", after which he moves away. Then there is the dissolute Herod, with whom Jesus does not speak at all. We also have Nicodemus, whom we have already mentioned and who can be taken as an example of another type of man. And we have Saul, who starts out as a cruel persecutor, and then becomes the Apostle Paul. In the Gospel there are also many other men to whom Jesus says, "Follow me," and whose reaction is different from that of the rich young man. Unlike him they obey . . . and there are a great many of these, too.

My dear sons, Christ says, "Follow me," to each person, to each young man. He says, "Follow me," to each one of us. And following him means walking after him, in his footsteps, following him with your mind, your will and the whole of yourself.

You may imagine that this means not following yourself, but that is in fact just what it does mean. This is most important for us, since each of us wants above all to follow himself. Following Christ also means following yourself. Christ does not tear you away from yourselves. He does not diminish or nullify the personhood of any of us. He enriches us if we truly desire to join him and shoulder the responsibility we have in common with all humanity: "Go therefore and make disciples of all nations." The Kingdom of God is something which involves everybody, and this is why every man who seeks the Kingdom of God finds himself.

Amen

7. Conversion

A person cannot be beyond good and evil, which is, however, where Nietzsche tried to place him. Only God is beyond or, rather, above good and evil, whereas each person finds himself constantly between good and evil. Being between good and evil is our natural condition, but it also means that we are with Christ, because in a certain sense, as we have seen in the past few days, he himself stood between good and evil.

When reflecting on the Gospel, which is the divine revelation referring to human things, we have noted that its content is divided between positive and negative situations. We saw in particular that there was much sin around Christ in the Gospel, which is why our interior attitude, or our position with Christ, must constitute our starting point.

It is an illusion if any of us thinks he is beyond good and evil or beyond morality. There is no such situation, and there is no way of creating one.

We must look at things realistically, and religion always has a deeply realistic viewpoint, even if some people may try to convince you that *religious* means *idealistic* in an imprecise sense of the word.

A realistic view of humanity, which is based on the Gospel and comes from a position at Christ's side, lies precisely in the fact that man stands constantly between good and evil and must therefore try to find the right path between them.

We have seen that there are powerful (although maybe this is not the most precise description) and intense forces or energies of sin within us. We have also seen that sin is not a question of a single moment or simply of an isolated act. Sin cannot be like this, because it is a transgression of the divine law which our intellect informs us of and which God himself has laid down for us; sin is the actual moment of transgression, and when we confess our sins we normally confess those moments when we committed these transgressions.

However, we saw that sin must be sought beyond this moment—both before and after it. When a person violates the will of God and at a given moment commits a sin, this is because certain forces of sin are acting both within him and also on him from outside. The influence of these forces of evil and sin, which come from outside man and act on him, constitute what is called temptation, what Christ called the spirit of the world or the spirit of darkness.

These energies act within each of us, and we can each of us easily recognize certain tendencies to evil within himself. We would be naive or ingenuous, or frankly deluded and totally lacking in self-knowledge, if we denied the existence of such tendencies and inclinations to evil within us.

We certainly do have them within us, and they are so closely linked with our nature that we often tend to put the blame for our sins on our nature itself. We say that it is our nature which pushes us toward sin. However, this is only partly true: the forces of sin are indeed linked with the forces of nature within us, but they are not identical with them since, if this were so, man would be nothing but sin; and this is not the case.

The forces of nature also work within us against sin, and the first of these anti-sin forces is our human conscience. I have already mentioned the conscience in passing. Today I want to say something more, and to state first of all that it is a real energy or force of our nature or essence; it is an energy in the sense that it is able to rouse us. Our conscience manages to shake us from within in a way no human word from outside can do, and as not even the most gifted human preacher can do. Our conscience must be vigorous and resolute. It cannot afford to be indulgent, and it must be able to sum up a situation immediately. It must also have perseverance.

We know that most of the major works of world literature center around the question of the conscience. The Greek tragedies and Shakespeare's plays are all concerned with the conscience, because this force of nature is such a characteristic human feature.

Our conscience operates to overcome the forces of evil within us, so that we cannot claim that our nature urges us only toward evil. This would be a pessimistic exaggeration, because even if certain inclinations in our nature urge us toward evil, our conscience draws us away from it. Our conscience expresses itself by drawing us away from that evil.

Our conscience is constantly telling us what not to do. However, it also tells us what we should do. It commands some things and prohibits others. It draws us away from evil, and when sin has already taken place, if our conscience is a true, vigorous one, it immediately sums up the situation.

Our conscience judges us. Through it, man judges himself before any other human court is able to do so. Our conscience judges us, and this judicial function is a great ally of what is good. This fundamental energy of our personality does not only draw us away from evil, but actually urges us toward good.

My dear children, no psychoanalytical technique can take the place of the conscience, although it is certainly very important to bring those things which have accumulated in our subconscious out into the open and into our conscious mind, because this brings order to the chaos of the past which we carry within ourselves.

Our conscience works in the same way, trying to lead us out of chaos and to bring order to everything found within us and restore a balance to our whole interior set of experiences and actions. However, the work of the conscience is not confined to knowledge or to bringing things to our attention and rearranging them. Virtue and morality are not merely knowledge. Our conscience urges us on toward the good; and it would be a great misfortune if, despite our knowledge, it did not show us the decisions we should take. People weighed down by sin are moved to virtue by their conscience—and this is something which no amount of psychoanalysis can bring about.

The conscience is an energy and not only knowledge, and so it urges us toward the good, and it would be truly terrible for us if we had no way of finding this path that leads away from evil and toward good.

Even so, we must remember that evil persists within the person. Unfortunately, people often support a conception of morality which is so simplistic that it ignores the interior life of the person altogether. Serious crimes are punished through the penal system, with sentences to jails or concentration camps, and this is how people try to prevent theft, murder and prostitution. This narrow and restrictive conception of morality is defective: it is not yet true morality, which is linked to the interior person and to the energies of the conscience. Our conscience urges us toward good, and we would be truly wretched, and our situation literally hellish, if we were moved by our conscience but were unable to move away from evil and back toward good.

Religious—or, more precisely, Christian—morality is the only type of morality capable of effectively fulfilling our yearning for good. I do not know if you have ever listened to the Psalms being sung in church. Maybe the best known of them is Psalm 51, which begins with the words, "Have mercy on me, O God." You may not be familiar with the circumstances in which this psalm was written by King David. The story is told in Chapter 11 of the Second Book of Samuel.

What happened was that King David, who was a deeply religious man, succumbed to his passion for the wife of Uriah, one of his military officers who was at that time away at the front fighting and whose wife had therefore been left alone at home. David's passion led him to order her to come to him and to commit adultery with her. He was so blinded by his passion that he ordered Uriah's death, so that he would have greater freedom for this liaison.

However, this king, who was really a very religious man and who had sinned so gravely, had a sudden change of heart. And it was at that point that he wrote the psalm that begins "Have mercy on me." The lines which best sum up the whole psalm are: "Against thee, thee only, have I sinned; and done that which is evil in thy sight." These two phrases clarify the whole situation and show us the direction in which the workings of his conscience were moving and directing the man.

David's conscience suddenly awoke within him and urged him toward God, helping him to re-establish his relationship with him. Suddenly it is a question of *I* and *Thou*: "Against thee only have I sinned."

My dear children, this is not some sort of cruelty on the part of our conscience, but springs from the instinct of survival linked with the conscience. We can free ourselves of sin and extricate ourselves from it only by entering into the Thou-I I-Thou relationship. There is no other way of escaping from evil.

David saw the magnitude of the evil of his two actions of adultery and murder, and this awareness must have overwhelmed him in his innermost depths, so that he cried out: "I have done that which is evil in thy sight." If he had remained alone with his evil and sin, it would have destroyed him. However, when he became aware of having committed evil before God and realized that God was in a certain way aware of this evil, he felt ashamed and humiliated; but it was also a sense of relief and a help to him. This is the basic direction in which our conscience leads each one of us.

We can understand the great value of religion when we stand before God in order to re-establish this I-Thou relationship and, like David, say, "Against thee only . . . ," because only God can help me and free me from evil. All this is very wonderful and constitutes the greatness of religion; it is the greatness of that faith which is so often disparaged and despised. Something like what happened to David must take place within each of us: "Against thee only have I sinned." It is easy to destroy, reject or belittle the person, but we must not do so.

With David's "Have mercy on me, O God" in mind, it is easy to understand that the essence of the sacrament of Penance is, and must be, contrition. Contrition is not the same as fear, but is something broader and deeper; it is not simply fear before a threatening God.

On the other hand, our situation in sin would become extremely dangerous without God. As I have already said, we can each of us refuse God and stand outside his influence. When we reject God we are making him reject us: and this is what hell is. It is difficult to imagine, but the situation of the person who has fallen into sin and who remains there without God gives a clear picture of this. He has nobody to whom he can say, "I have sinned against thee"; he does not have that unique, great *Thee* who can help him at this moment.

My dear ones, as regards sin, we must take up the position of children. Only their father can help them as regards the human order and human relationships. Similarly, only the Father can help us when we have sinned, and in this way repentance is not so very difficult. How many times in your life have you felt that only your father or your mother could help you?

In cases where this approach does not waken an attitude of repentance, we have another starting point in the suffering Christ. It is amazing how far God is willing to wait for us, and this attitude is summed up and expressed in the Christ of the passion. If other feelings do not arouse your soul, compassion will surely do so. Here we are not concerned with whether people's sufferings in concentration camps or prisons have been lesser or greater than those of Christ at his scourging or on Calvary. What does concern us is the fact that each time we approach Christ being scourged or Christ on Calvary there is a real possibility that something will be stirred in us and we shall change.

"The whole Christ" is placed for our conversion—in order to convert us and constantly arouse in us the attitude of a child who says, "Father, forgive me! Father, help me!" This is Christ.

If we find contrition difficult, then we should try and listen to the voice of our hearts. We should try to do the Way of the Cross slowly, from one station to the next, each of us in his or her own personal way. We do not necessarily need a prayer book, for it may not tell us very much, or at the most it will describe what takes place at each station; instead, each of us should go personally to the place where he fell under the weight of the cross, the place where he was stripped of his garments, the place where he was nailed to the cross, and the place where he began his final agony. We must draw closer and closer, and linger there, gazing at him.

Christ is God himself, who continues to convert people, even on the Way of the Cross: we see this process of conversion in Simon of Cyrene, the women of Jerusalem, and Veronica. The Way of the Cross is the perfect school for contrition. Sometimes our problems with regard to confession spring from the fact that we cannot resolve to resist sin in the future. How can we know if we shall change, when appearances would tend to indicate that we shall remain the same? In fact, we can maybe already feel the forces of evil stirring in us again and urging us back toward sin.

The conscience raises us up, and the forces of evil drag us down.

My dear children, the resolution not to sin any more is first and foremost a matter of conversion to God; it is not a matter of being certain that one will not commit the same sin again, but rather of the will not to do so. We should cling to God with our whole will. We would not be capable of bringing about this great transformation on our own, but if we cling to God, if we cling to Christ, if we stay close to him, it will gradually take place within us.

These are long-term processes. We tend to approach the religious and moral life with too little patience, as if it were a matter of something like a surgical operation or an injection, which will immediately make us better again. Change is a long-term process. The forces of sin act around and within us, and we need to make a systematic and carefully supervised effort if we are to transform and weaken them. Our nature and conscience work in this direction; and, above all, grace works in this direction.

Grace is also an energy—a force which tends to keep man close to God and to transform him inwardly, ennobling him. It is therefore important for us to learn how to release the energy of grace within ourselves. This is in large part the work of the sacramental life. Confession serves to release the energy of grace within us. And, my dear ones, what we need in order for all this to take place is prayer. Prayer is the simplest and most widely practiced way of releasing the energies of grace—those forces which lead to victory over sin and its forces—within us.

We have already clearly established that prayer is conversation in the I-Thou relationship. Prayer is effective in preparing us for the sacrament of Penance, because it means establishing the contact between *I* and *Thou*. As conversation, prayer brings this about right from the start.

Apart from this, if prayer is conversation with God, we must always remember who it is we are speaking with and address him with deep respect, a spirit of praise and an attitude of humility. "Who am I who stand before Thy face?" "Dust and nothing," wrote Mickiewicz, with humility.*

Conversation is an art. Anybody who engages in conversation must not talk about himself without pausing for breath, because this would not be a conversation but simply a monologue. Although we must talk about ourselves a great deal in prayer, we must also allow the Lord to speak. Of course God's way of speaking to us is different from our way, but he does speak to us, and his words are intelligible; they are interior factors closely linked to the unremitting work of our conscience. Grace strengthens the work of the conscience and this manifests itself through prayer.

People often say that they do not know how to pray; but prayer is a simple matter. I would above all emphasize that the important thing is to pray, in whatever form, even if you just recite the prayers you were taught as a child. Pray, however you do it, because this is what is important. Never say

---

*Adam Mickiewicz (1798–1855), Polish poet and dramatist.

that you do not pray because you do not know how to, because this is not true. We all know how to pray. The words of prayer are simple, and the rest follows of itself. If you say you do not know how to pray you are deceiving yourself—and maybe someone else as well. This is poverty of spirit and a lack of good will and courage. You must pray, however you do it, and it does not matter whether you use a prayer book or whether you recite your prayers by heart.

You can also pray with your mind. When we find ourselves in contact with nature we pray in a perfect manner. A person immersed in the world of nature finds that it almost speaks for him and to him.

The most complete prayer is undoubtedly the Holy Mass. In it, the greatness of prayer enfolds and fill us, but on the one condition that we learn to participate in it and are not simply "present" in some corner of the church, maybe listening to what the priest has to say and then going on our way.

I assure you that if you make an effort to participate, the Holy Mass, with its prayer, will slowly fill you to overflowing. Then you will not say that you do not know how to pray or that prayer is boring. You will be filled with Christ's prayer, and the precise words and prayer methods you use will become secondary in the face of the real experience of being filled with the prayer of Christ.

I cannot urge you enough to learn to participate in the Holy Mass and not simply to be present. You should participate with your mind, heart, will, and sin. Yes, with your sins, too. At the beginning of the Mass we confess our sins, which is like saying, "I have sinned against thee."

We must persevere in this attitude, which is to some extent in crisis among young people today, and we should remember that Christ told us that by our perseverance we should save our souls (cf. Luke 21:19). We are often very impatient when it comes to the spiritual life. We want everything immediately; we want everything to be ready and easy.

If we say too much about ourselves when we talk to God, he cannot say anything to us. The same thing applies if we are always asking him for things. However, it is through our perseverance that we shall save our souls. My dear children, it is your souls which are at stake here.

Will you save your souls? We have almost reached the end of our retreat and you must by now have learned something about this subject. The questions you should be asking yourselves are these: Am I saving my soul? Do I know something about it? Am I in control of it? Am I capable of guiding it in the right direction? Will I be able to guide it to the point where the I-Thou relationship is established?

We all hope this for ourselves. We hope that we can save our souls, so that we may not provide the ground within us for that chaos which debilitates us and leaves us with the impression that our life is aimless—so that the chaos which poisons our soul may not take root, because even if we do maybe pretend to make the best of it, it is still not a happy situation.

Will you save your souls? Only Christ told you where you could do this. I would express the most important prayer of these days as follows: "O Christ, who told us that we should save our souls through our perseverance, help us to do this; help us to save our souls so that we do not perish."

My dear children, during this retreat I have tried to the best of my ability to highlight the underlying questions of God and the soul, Christ and the Gospel.

If I may now be permitted to ask something of you, I would beg you, for your part, to do everything that lies within your power. You see, what I have told you is only a sort of reflection, whereas the reality is what must take place in and through you.

Today many of you came to confession and to communion, and I would ask you to do the same tomorrow. It will be possible to go to confession throughout the day, and then the retreat will close with a celebration of the Mass. I would ask all of you to participate. In these few days we have formed a community, and this community should reach its fulfillment when we all gather at the Lord's table tomorrow for Holy Communion.

I should like to make a further suggestion. Easter comes in a few days, so try to make an effort to spend these holy days with Christ. In the Christian life today everything is based on the Eucharist or, more simply, on Christ. So make an effort to receive him in the next few days too—on Holy Thursday and Good Friday and on Easter Day—so that this retreat does not simply leave a vague impression but is the start of something new within you.

It is normal for anyone giving a retreat to ask one more thing at the end. He must, like Christ, be careful not to issue orders or make claims; he must use gentle methods, because each person has been provided with free will.

So, if I may ask you something at the end, it is that you should be more united with Christ after this retreat. May the Holy Communion you receive tomorrow be an expression of your relationship with him for your future life as well.

Amen

8. Witness

Although Christ is present in the Gospel as Word, he is also present as Event, Act and Reality.

We have constantly tried to examine these moments beside Christ in order to find a place beside him for ourselves.

Christ is in fact the One who reveals and also the One who converts. He converts us to God, so that the Gospel may be fulfilled in all its breadth and so that its central reality—the relationship between the divine Self and the human self, between God and man—may be brought to fulfillment. The invisible God, the personal God, wants to give himself to us. This is a supernatural fact which is beyond our comprehension without the help of faith. This is why Christ instituted the Eucharist, through which God's self-giving to the human soul was made a sacrament. When we are about to receive communion, there is good reason to call to mind Christ's great courage.

We have analyzed the Gospel and seen that he is always between good and evil and not "beyond" them. We, with our sin, are close to him, and he wants to enter into us and into our lives in order to be able to work within us, where our fundamental decisions are taken, and to urge us along the path to good. He wants to draw us away from evil and sin and set us on the path of righteousness, with that tremendous energy it engenders and which he possesses.

We have spoken of the forces of sin and nature, and more

particularly of those of the conscience; we have also discussed the forces of grace, which are inseparable from Christ and are bound up with his great courage in coming to me. Despite the fact that I am drawn towards sin, he comes to me, places himself within me between good and evil, and trusts in me. At this point we may be led to exclaim: "O Christ, how very courageous you are!"

My dear children, love has great courage and does not spare itself. Christ did not spare himself in the land of Galilee. He said of himself that, while foxes had holes and birds of the air had nests, he had nowhere to lay his head (cf. Matthew 8:20; Luke 9:58). He was constantly on the move, hounded and persecuted, sometimes spending whole nights in prayer, and in the end he went unresisting to his passion and death. He did not spare himself. And all this was always and only for my sake.

Love is fearless and does not spare itself. Today Christ is still courageous in his love; he still does not spare himself and constantly gives himself to mankind, to me. "Lord, I am not worthy" (Matthew 8:8): this is all we can say, before falling silent.

This is constantly taking place through Christ, because he is constantly creating us, coming to us sacramentally and creating us from within, to the extent that we allow and in accord with the opportunities we provide. There are some people who allow themselves to be created to an exceptional degree and so he transforms them radically, while there are others who do not open themselves to him and are not willing to allow him to work within them. There are still others who open themselves a small way; however, this little chink is enough for him to enter into the person and transform him at least to that extent. Christ creates in a way all his own, because he loves.

My dear children, we are not only witnesses, but are also

objects of the work of creation which Christ carries out within us. Today in Holy Communion he wants to create us anew and transform us. However, there is a second aspect of this situation, inasmuch as we too create Christ. This is not an empty expression, for the Christ we create is known as the Church. We often hear it said that the Church is the mystical body of Christ and that we are part of it; we are its components, or, if we want to retain the analogy, its cells. So we can say in a certain sense that he depends on all of us. The mystical body of Christ, the Church, depends on us; it is our creation or our work. The action begins with him: he creates us, and we, who have been created divinely by him, in turn create him, the Church.

My dear ones, we create him first and foremost through the witness we bear him. I have said this in different contexts in the past few days. We create Christ above all because we bear witness to him.

The first people who confessed Christ were witnesses of Christ in the sense that they had actually seen him: "We have seen him, we have seen his works, we have heard his words, we have seen him after his resurrection, and we have seen his glory when he ascended into heaven."

The word *martyr* (which means "witness" in Greek) has taken on a very deep significance in the Church: a martyr is a person who bears witness, and the Church, inasmuch as it is a community of men, exists through their confession of and witness to Christ.

The Church has great esteem for the role of the martyr, and confirms this at Mass. You may have been struck by the fact that at Mass the priest bends and kisses the altar. He does this because the altar contains relics of martyrs who bore witness to Christ with their death, right from the earliest centuries when there were as yet no churches and Mass was celebrated on the tombs of the martyrs in the catacombs. When the Church emerged from the catacombs, it retained this custom. Even if it is not a proper tomb, each altar with its relics is a little sepulcher. There is therefore deep significance in the fact that the priest kisses the altar—or reliquary—and then turns to the people with the words, "The Lord be with you." This gesture establishes deep communion between those martyrs who bore witness to Christ and us who bear witness to Christ and who are present in church at Mass in order to do so. This, my dear children, is what the Church is.

The Church was organized from within by Christ himself, who said to Peter: "You are Peter, and on this rock I will build my church, and the powers of death shall not prevail against it. I will give you the keys of the kingdom of heaven, and whatever you bind on earth shall be bound in heaven, and whatever you loose on earth shall be loosed in heaven" (Matthew 16:18–19), and to the Apostles: "Go therefore and teach all nations, . . . and lo, I am with you always, to the end of the world" (Matthew 28:19).

Christ has organized the Church from within once and for all. As a human society it is regenerated and lasts through the centuries because Christ constantly creates it and organizes it from within as his own mystical body. And this takes place because of us, because of what Christ carries out within us. Thus Christ creates us and we create him, that is, the Church.

My dear children, in its final destiny, the Church is of necessity like Christ. Christ told those first witnesses, his Apostles: "A disciple is not above his teacher" (Matthew 10:24); "A servant is not greater than his master. If they persecuted me, they will persecute you; if they kept my word, they will keep yours also" (John 15:20). All this applies to us too.

Thus Christ established once and for all the destiny of

the Church, binding it to his own, because he knew that it would be a struggle to fulfill what the Gospel had brought to humanity. However, when he foretold persecution and obstacles he also said that the final victory belongs to him and to the Church. "If they listen to my words, they will listen to yours also." How wonderful and how true this whole concept is! And how full of both divine and human meaning! In it, with the help of Christ in the Church, each of us can discover its application to himself as an individual as well as its divine significance. I hope that this discovery constitutes the fruit of your participation in this retreat, and that you will continue to act in accordance with it in the future as well.

Ending our retreat means receiving Holy Communion, uniting ourselves with Christ sacramentally, and I do hope you will go to meet him and be received by him. "Accept me, take me back, because I have maybe been wandering or lost, because I am confused or in doubt. Take me and guide me." Speak to him with sincerity but also with clarity and conviction. Do not be afraid to talk with him, even when he tells you the truth about yourselves, however unpalatable. He is not afraid of the truth, and no truth about man is too frightful for him, because he can place his own truth and wealth in each human truth; he can always place his love in every human truth, and before the power of love everything else loses its power.

So you should say to Christ: "Take me back again, accept me back again."

At the end of Mass, I want to give to all of you who have taken part in this retreat a blessing which, under the conditions of confession and communion, imparts an indulgence, so that you can accomplish what you have meditated on in the course of these days.

Amen

Part Two:

Christ Within Us

A retreat for university students
Cracow, 1972

1. Prayer

In the name of the Father, and of the Son, and of the Holy Spirit. Amen.

Praised be Jesus Christ!

I should like to begin this retreat by asking you a very simple question. I ask this same question of everybody, including myself, but at this point I am asking *you*: Do you pray?

I could have led up to this question gradually, and asked it at the end of the retreat, and I did in fact wonder whether I should ask it now or later. However, I am asking it at the beginning because it constitutes the very heart of a retreat.

A retreat means leaving the turmoil of everyday life and gathering oneself in recollection. One can recollect the self or meditate on the self, which are two different methods. However, in a retreat we are dealing with recollection, that is, removing ourselves from the dispersiveness of life, so that we can establish a link with God.

And contact with God means prayer! Prayer can take on various forms, but it is always contact with God and means leaving dispersiveness behind us and entering into recollection—not in order to be alone, but in order to be close to him.

A retreat always means opening oneself, even if in some ways I shut myself into my thoughts, experiences, consciousness and past life. I open myself to God to the degree that I manage to isolate myself.

These reflections are what led me to start by asking if you pray. This question is undoubtedly the key to a retreat and to the Christian life, and we shall not deal with it here in abstract terms.

I should also like to ask you a second question, which is linked to the first: Why do you pray? Why do I pray? Why do we pray? Why? We shall be concerned mainly with this second question today. And if you do not pray, the question would be: Why not? If this is your interior, spiritual situation, we must look for the answer to this latter question, because there can be a number of possible reasons, since the lack of prayer can mean many different things.

It can simply mean that you have outgrown childhood prayers, just as you have outgrown children's clothes, and that you have not yet put on an adult's clothes. It can also means a certain lack of form or methods or expression; in these cases little effort has usually been made to find the means of expression for prayer.

The lack of prayer can never be taken to mean that you do not need prayer. Indeed, the longer we do not pray, the greater the need grows, so that at a certain moment it explodes in the search for some outlet.

Not praying does not necessarily mean that we do not feel the need to pray. In this case your prayer needs a more interior basis, a more spiritual attitude, and a deeper orientation; you must simply look for the means of expression, and the type of prayer which corresponds with and satisfies your university intellect and your mature moral personality.

I have added this rider to the discussion, since we all come on retreat in order to re-examine the basic question of prayer and of our relationship of trust with God and openness to him. We come on retreat because we already do pray or because we want to learn to do so.

Let us return to the basic question and main subject of

today's meditation: Why do we pray? Why does everybody pray—Christians, Moslems, Buddhists, pagans? Why do even those who do not think they are praying pray?

The answer is very simple: I pray because God exists. I know that God exists, and this is why I pray. Some people will give this type of frank reply: "I know that God exists." However, others may phrase their answer differently, with somewhat less certainty: "I believe," or maybe even, "I'm searching." In the course of this reflection, I should like you to become more precise in the use of these different expressions, since they describe a variety of different spiritual attitudes.

We can ask how you know God exists. I am put in mind of a letter which I received a long time ago from a naturalist and which had a deep effect on me. I shall have to quote from memory, since I have lost the original letter. However, I shall remember it till my dying day: "I do not find God specifically in the course of my scientific work. But there are moments—and these happen most often in the face of the majesty of nature, for example when looking at the mountains and their beauty—when something strange happens to me: in the course of my scientific work I do not find God, but in those moments I feel absolutely certain that he exists, and then I begin to pray." I think that many present-day intellectuals would express themselves in a similar way.

How do I know that God exists? There are a number of logical arguments, but they have fallen into disuse, so that people today tend to feel that they have no place in their ways of thinking and understanding. Even so, Einstein's words always spring to mind, and I shall have to quote from memory again, so that they may not be quite exact: "Penetrating the secrets of nature and explaining them scientifically shows us that everything was conceived in a wonderful manner; it to some extent reveals to us the thought and wisdom of the 'other part'—of that which is 'beyond' and 'above' what is found within the realm of our experience and cognitive research."

I have often thought that this way of describing the truth about God is very similar to the first words of Saint John's Gospel: "In the beginning was the Word." The Word as visible reality, and as accessible to our experience and knowledge, indicates what was in the beginning, that with which this reality must of necessity be explained. *Word* means thought, knowledge, mind.

Here is man, a part of that visible reality which attracts him and stimulates his ever increasing interest and the impulse to find out more, which urges him on to find a satisfactory answer. This man—one can say "this word" with a small *w*, this intellect, a part of the whole visible reality—is united, precisely through this reality and its richness and depth, with the Word—with this intelligence, thought and intellect without which the richness, complexity and precision of the world, which is moreover filled with constant unexpected factors, becomes incomprehensible. Even so, scientists of only a few decades ago thought that everything could be fully explained within the categories then at their disposal. Today, we no longer think like this.

Then there is the path of reason: from the need to know more and to embrace the totality, everywhere and in every dimension, it constantly asks questions as to origin and causes, in order to work its way back to the first cause.

On the Search for the First Cause is the title of a book written by a famous philosopher which describes, among other things, the different methods used in this research and the various problems entailed.* We can state that the search for

---

*The author is most probably referring to the book by Jacques Maritain which appeared in English under the title *Approaches to God* (New York: Harper, 1954).

the first cause through human reason is simple, for the path which leads man from knowledge of the world to knowledge of its first cause appears simple. In the history of human knowledge and the history of thought, especially philosophical thought, this simple, straightforward, empirical path of the intellect towards God (*itinerarium mentis ad Deum*) has sometimes been complicated, and we can even say that it becomes more and more complicated in the field of human thought. However, this certainly does not mean that this way, with its basic simplicity, is always the same, for it can sometimes seem wider and sometimes narrower.

Why do you pray? Because I know that God exists, and because I am always seeking God.

My dear children, this whole path of human thought wends its way through different generations in many different ways towards the first cause, and a new light shines throughout all these studies, all this research and uncertainty: that light is the witness of Jesus Christ.

I pray because I believe. What does believing mean? Believing means bearing Jesus Christ's witness within oneself.

These two ways—that of thought which leads to God, and that of the witness of Jesus Christ (in other words, faith)—meet, join together and mingle within us. It is wise to distinguish between them so as to know what forms part of the one and what comes from the other, what is the work of human thought regarding God and what is the light of divine revelation to man.

We can understand the expression "witness of Jesus Christ" in a very specific and literal way. We all know who Jesus Christ was, and we know how he gave his witness, a witness made up of deeds and words, the testimony of a whole life that was unequivocally and totally turned towards the Father and given to mankind, right to the very end. The witness of Jesus Christ for which people would try to stone him and for which they would eventually crucify him, was that of saying that he was the Son of God.

This witness of Jesus Christ can be broadened to include all God's revelation to mankind from the beginning to the end. Thus the witness of Jesus Christ contains both the original revelation which we find in the first chapter of the book of Genesis, and also later revelation, linked to the history of the People of God in the Old Testament, that people he chose in order to communicate to humanity.

God certainly did speak through men and women with human words, despite the insuperable difference in levels between God's truth and human truth, divine thought and human thought. God managed to overcome this difference and found human expressions for his truth. He found them in his relationship with the chosen people of the Old Testament, and he found them finally in Jesus Christ: "The Word was made flesh" (John 1:14).

Jesus Christ is the culmination and fullness of revelation. In him, God tells man everything and speaks fully of himself. He speaks of everything which can be transferred from the level of divine thought and the divine Word to the level of human thought, speech and knowledge. All this is fully and completely found in Jesus Christ.

Believing means having the witness of Jesus Christ within oneself, and many people do have it. However, people have it and carry it within themselves in very different ways: Christians do so, as is clear from their name and from their baptism, but non-Christians also do so, in a different manner. Since the Second Vatican Council we have come to see this question more clearly and accept it with a more open mind.

So the way we must answer the question of why we pray is by affirming that God exists; we know he exists, we seek him out and believe in him. Some people today have expressed doubt as to whether the word *believe* is worthy of man. So consider whether it is worthy of mankind, and of each one of us, to believe and to carry Christ's witness within us. You must certainly have thought about this, but please give it some further thought. The purpose of a retreat is to examine these questions in greater depth.

The Gospel, the Good News, was revealed to us through Jesus Christ. Thanks to him we know not only that God exists but also that he is the first cause of everything which exists; we know who he is. In Jesus Christ's witness, understood in the broader sense, we know who God is, and this testimony embraces all of revelation from the very beginning.

So who is God? God is the Creator, and as Creator he is the Lord of what he has created. This truth is strongly imprinted in the human consciousness through the original revelation and dominates the Old Testament; and through Jesus Christ it is linked, from beginning to end, to the new truth that God is Father.

Father means the person who gives life: my father is the person who gave me life, together with my mother. God is Father and gives life, my life and all human life. To this extent he is only the Creator. However, he gives me his own life: I am conceived in the eternal Son, who became man so that I could become to some extent like him.

Our father is the person who gives us life, and God is Father; but he is also Redeemer. The Son pays for the paternity of his Father in each one of us, and in a certain sense ransoms the paternity of his Father for each of us. He places us within that reality which is called God.

This is the new dimension, the fullness of revelation, the Gospel which is identified with the witness of Jesus Christ. Christ gives each of us his Spirit, the Holy Spirit, so that we can cry out with inner certainty: "Father!" This exclamation must be backed with a great divine guarantee! Think how many people—and not only Christians—say, "Father!" How immense is Christ's action which has provided such a divine guarantee for human thought and words!

What does praying mean, and why should we pray? My dear children, I think we have now answered these questions in a broad sense. And in providing these answers we have tried to indicate the paths along which we move towards God and along which God approaches us. We have also tried to indicate the point at which this meeting takes place.

Prayer is conversation, and we are well aware that conversation can take various forms. Sometimes it is a simple exchange of words, and this is simply the exterior aspect. Deep conversation takes place when we exchange not only words but also thoughts, hearts and feelings, in other words, when we give of our own selves.

In its different forms, prayer takes place on different levels and at different depths: the Moslem prays, invoking his Allah with great pride wherever he may be at specified moments; the Buddhist prays, immersed and almost losing himself in contemplation; and the Christian prays, taking from Christ the word *Father*, for which he has a wonderful guarantee in his own spirit, through the Spirit of Christ.

In this way, when we pray all the different paths combine and form one single path. Inspiration comes to our minds and lips above all from the testimony of Jesus Christ, who teaches us to say, "Our Father."

Let us stop at this point for today, my dear children.

Let us accept the witness of Christ and with the help of these reflections let us repeat together the words which he himself taught us. In the course of our retreat, we shall discover their inner meaning, so that we come to understand that to which everything must be directed and from which everything must flow.

Let us say together: "Our Father. . . ."

Amen

2. Human Development

My dear children, yesterday we considered two questions about prayer. The first one (Do you pray?) will be the key question for the whole retreat. Let us place prayer at the center of our way of living this retreat, basing everything on it and referring everything back to it. The second one (Why do you pray?) gave us a chance to re-examine both the orientation of human thought and also the content of our faith, which together make up the basic reply to it. I pray because I believe that God exists.

We shall take a further look at the second question today. Yesterday we noted that prayer and its meaning are linked to knowledge of God, and today we shall try to see how all this is linked to human knowledge. We are faced with that basic concept which is as old as religion, as old as Christianity, and which Saint Augustine formulated admirably in the expression *"Noverim Te, noverim me"* ("I would know Thee, in order to know myself"). In this very concise phrase, God and man express not only two elements, but also the fundamental passions, concerns, hopes and aims of Christianity. God and man.

Saint Augustine also said, *"Deum et animam scire cupio,"* and in these words he expressed the same concept: that my greatest desire, my passion, is to know God and the soul.

Christianity is not only a religion but is also a humanism. It is significant that Scripture scholars devote quite a lot

of attention to discussing whether the Bible is a book mainly about God or one which contains God's thoughts about
humanity.

So when we consider why we pray, this question entails
a twofold attitude—toward God, and toward man—and
the delimitations and elements of these attitudes cannot be
separated.

The word *person* has great significance. Today our way of
thinking about people is defined by quantity, so that we
speak of nations, continents, humanity, expressing all this
in figures—so many thousands, so many millions, so many
billions. This quantitative way of looking at mankind dis-
guises the essence of things. The Gospel and Christianity
always direct us to the essence of things, because in the
midst of those thousands, millions and billions there is always the person, or, in other words, my specific, human
self, one and indivisible.

In reflection on mankind, Christianity and the Gospel
have always brought us back (and always will) from the nu-
merical aspect to the person, to that concrete, human self,
one and irreplaceable, which is found in a unique relationship with God. There is no other relationship which can define the person—this human *I*—in its unique and irreplaceable position as this relationship, this "meeting point" with
God, does. Person-God, God-person.

This concept is a feature of Christian thought; this new
content or attitude springs from prayer, because when we
pray the God-person, person-God relationship manifests itself as the most fundamental and most complete reality.

Person can mean many things. The person can be described and analyzed under many aspects, but in the end
any human method is ineffective when dealing with the reality of personhood.

History describes the events of society and nations, and

also the various great human figures as found in these events. However, it does not give the history of each person; my history, your history, the history of every person is an uncharted land, so that we can, with the great naturalist Alexis Carrel, say that man is "the unknown." We can describe man, but more as "resultant" or as the average. When we describe the person, we see him in development, and normally we begin at the beginning, so that we can give an outline of the history of each individual: as infant, small child, schoolchild, student, then as adult, parent, professional person, in full possession of his capacities, and, finally, in old age.

If we base our description solely on the physical aspect, it is easy to see a downward curve. We know that the individual does not grow only visibly, but also that his or her forces increase to a certain point, reach a zenith, and then start to decrease. Although they may follow different patterns, physical development is accompanied by development of the psychological functions, which are linked to the senses as a whole and to the richness of the emotions; sense perception and emotional sensitivity also grow, are refined, and then weaken and atrophy.

The development of thought, knowledge and intellectual ability takes place on a deeper level in the person. A great deal of growth takes place between the first words and the first childish ideas, the first naive questions which sometimes concern important subjects, and later stages of study, when the mind comes to understand trigonometry, literary analysis, philosophical reflection or mathematical logic. All this is part of human development.

We must view each individual person from this angle. Even the less gifted people with whom we sometimes meet belong to this great human reality of the person in development.

We must not limit ourselves to consideration of the phenomena of development, but must try to find their source, their hidden causes. We must investigate the origins of these phenomena and what underlies them, and the basis of ways of thinking, deciding and choosing. Knowledge about the human person is thus enriched with concepts such as those of the intellect, reason and free will, and thus with the faculties of self-determination and choice.

Experts in the field no doubt could—or would—fill out the picture of the person in development that I have sketched in a rather summary and fragmentary fashion. However, this person in development is described definitively in the first chapter of the book of Genesis: "God created man in his own image and likeness" (1:27). But is this really so? Is each individual person, each human self, best described by the words "the image and likeness of God"? This is the key question.

It is not possible to integrate the person fully in other contexts or dimensions. This is not to deny the truth of man's link with nature and of his resemblance to the world which has from ancient times been known as the "animal world." It merely shows that the person is not fully part of this latter context but possesses something more—and it is this "something more" which defines him.

This "something more" can be approached from various angles, and there is no time here to talk about the whole theory of the human phenomenon. Since this is a spiritual retreat, I should like to concentrate on one specific aspect of this "something more" which defines everything; the aspect in question is the conscience.

The person is in fact conscience; and if we do not grasp this central factor of conscience it is impossible to examine or discuss human development. The conscience provides the basis for the definitive structure and defines me as that unique and unrepeatable self or *I*.

Let us take as an example those events we have heard so much about in the past few months, that is, what took place at Auschwitz between Maximilian Kolbe and his executioners. Both Kolbe and his executioners were human beings, each with a human conscience. And what forms did this conscience take in the two cases? On the one hand we have the one which must be acclaimed, admired and accepted by the judgment of all mankind and which must be placed in its treasury for all times; while on the other hand we have a type of person or human being which everybody, independently of any religious faith, must reject and repudiate—or reject as far as possible, since even here we are concerned with a human person.

The greatness of the person in development is linked on the deepest level to his conscience. However, when we consider the person in development we cannot think solely of his beginnings, because that will never allow us to describe the development and full evolution of the person. We must also look at his purpose or end or, in other words, final reality—or, to use the Greek term, eschatology. This end is death. The processes of human development cannot be properly described if we do not start with the end, that is, with death; and this applies also in the case of Father Kolbe, whom I took as an example. We must start with death if we want to describe the full development of the person. But is death the person's full eschatology? Is it in fact the definitive reality? The materialistic ideology of the world in fact sees death as the definitive reality, so that not only is a person's life a constant movement towards death, but he also lives within the limitations of death, beyond which there is nothing.

The book of Genesis tells us that "You are dust, and to dust you will return" (3:19), and we remember these words of the Creator every Ash Wednesday. But if the person's eschatology or ultimate reality is death, what happens to the conscience and to that which has been developed in the person? Will they lead towards the figure represented by Maximilian Kolbe or that represented by his executioners? What will become of the conscience and of everything it has formed in each of us throughout all the years of our lives from the first moments when we could discern between good and evil? What will become of all this richness or, alternatively, of all this wretchedness? What is the point if the person simply develops towards death, and ends there?

Even supposing one accepted his ideology of the world, I do not know if Marx would have been right in claiming that man is the root of everything. Maybe Sartre was nearer the truth when he said that man aspires to that which he defines as "God"—even if, he adds, this is an empty word, so that it is "a useless passion."

Even so, if we consider everything we have within us and analyze only one single process—that of the conscience—it will be difficult, without denying that man is the root, to accept that he develops solely towards death, because he also develops towards judgment. Judgment is one of the four last things the catechism tells us to keep in mind. The person develops towards that judgment which is the beginning of eternal life.

The book of Genesis tells us that "God created man in his image and likeness" and adds that he placed him before the tree of the knowledge of good and evil. This is obviously a symbolic expression, but it is also very realistic, since it is a great truth that man is placed before the tree of the knowledge of good and evil, that he finds himself between good and evil, that he must constantly choose, and that choice, decisions and actions have value (are good) or have a non-value (are evil). Human life is lived between good and evil.

This is where we can see the grandeur of human life. Human beings possess greatness because they can choose, so that in a certain sense even sin testifies that they are great. I am not saying that it testifies to their greatness, just as we cannot say that the actions of the Auschwitz executioners testify to their greatness; however, in a certain sense even sin does testify that human beings are great. If this were not so, it would be difficult to understand God's whole relationship with them, with these people who stand between good and evil. God did not cut himself off from mankind because of the tree of the knowledge of good and evil, even though we know that the human race has often exceeded the bounds of this tree. This factor, which is found in the history of mankind and of society, but above all in that of each individual person, has not affected the Creator's great concern for the person who chooses, falls, sins, and rises again. God goes out towards the person, not only as judge, but as Father seeking his prodigal son; he is our guide and places his commandments along our road as sure guideposts.

We know the Old Testament commandments which were given to Moses, mostly in the form of prohibitions: "You shall not kill, you shall not commit adultery, you shall not steal, you shall not bear false witness," and so on. All these prohibitions from God are limits which we must not exceed. All humanity—every society and every system—is well aware that these prohibitions from God must not be altered, ignored or eliminated. We are all well aware of this fact.

We also know the New Testament, the Gospel, which gives us the ethic of the eight Beatitudes followed by men like Maximilian Kolbe. Many others, even in our city, have followed these Beatitudes, and there will always be others who will follow them.

Lastly, we know the commandment which summarizes and goes beyond all the others, the commandment of the love of God and neighbor, which Christ brought us as the ultimate word of this concern of the Judge and Father toward our human conscience.

In the course of a retreat conscience is always the central issue. If I said yesterday that the central issue was prayer, this was in order to bring you to what I am now saying today. Even our Lord Jesus was saying the same thing when he told us: "Not every one who says to me, 'Lord, Lord,' shall enter the kingdom of heaven, but he who does the will of my Father" (Matthew 7:21).

So in the course of this retreat we must focus our whole attention on this issue, bearing in mind that for each one of us we are dealing here with the culminating element which defines and expresses our selfhood and our human and personal dignity. This culminating element opens the person to God, bringing us close to him and uniting us with him. In the quest for this we must, through prayer, unceasingly concentrate the attention of our mind and will on our conscience.

My dear listeners, yesterday we closed our meditation by reciting the Lord's Prayer. I think that today it would be a good thing to choose the Ten Commandments as our evening prayer. Together we shall call to mind God's commandments and crown the recitation with the great commandment of love given to us by Christ:

I am the Lord your God, who brought you out of the land of Egypt, out of the house of bondage.

You shall have no other gods besides me.

You shall not take the name of the Lord your God in vain.

Remember the sabbath day, to keep it holy.
Honor your father and mother.
You shall not kill.
You shall not commit adultery.
You shall not steal.
You shall not bear false witness.
You shall not covet your neighbor's wife.
You shall not covet anything that is your neighbor's.

(Exodus 20:2–17)

Love is the fulfilling of the law.

(Romans 13:10)

You shall love the Lord your God with all your heart, and
with all your soul, and with all your mind.

(Matthew 22:37)

Amen

3. Love

We have meditated on Christ as witness of God, his Father and our Father, and then on Christ as witness of mankind and of the human conscience and the dignity of the human person. In this sense, the focus of our attention so far has been on the person, the human self or "I."

We shall now turn our attention to the community, the human "we." We shall speak of Christ as witness of this human community. It was he who spoke the greatest commandment in the history of mankind: the commandment of love. It could be fully guaranteed only by his lips. And it was with this commandment of love that Christ became the witness of the human community, because love has the function of uniting. In human beings, love is so great that it gives form to our interior being and determines the nature of our actions; and at the same time it unites people with one another, giving form to the human community.

Love is the Gospel commandment, but it also constitutes a problem for us.

Love is the center of human life. In it we can discern the creative force and also realize the meaning of this force and its creative quality, taking its absence as a starting point.

The absence of love leads to destruction and failure. It may be helpful to link the truth of love and of its absence (in other words, its opposite) with the history of our country. This year [1972] marks the second centenary of the first partition of Poland, and this event, which was the first of a series (although maybe not the first in the whole history of our nation), is closely linked with love—or, rather, with its absence. Some two hundred years before this event, the great Skarga* criticized his contemporaries for their pursuit of their own personal interests. But in these next two centuries exclusive interest in one's own prosperity and well-being, and the loss of any social conscience and love, increased to such an extent that by the late eighteenth century those who were directly responsible for running the country had lost all sense of their own duties and responsibilities. Today, a further two centuries later, it is still difficult to read about those events in novels and historical works without being deeply moved. Modern writers understand even more clearly the events of two hundred years ago which led to the loss of independence and the downfall of the country. And we all know what heroic efforts were needed later on. That excessive private and personal interest and that lack of love had to be redeemed with infinite love, in order to restore the country's independence.

I have recalled these things as an example to show the importance of love in human life and how it binds the components of the various human "we"s together; it provides a basis and gives strength to the human "we" in its various dimensions, and hinders and destroys everything which opposes it. Our nation is in fact a great human "we."

Love has various dimensions, and it also has different "circles" which encompass that great truth which motivates and builds up love and which hinders and destroys whatever stands in its way. This great truth, which Dante recognized too, is simply the translation into the different periods and dimensions of human life of the evangelical principle

---

*Piotyr Skarga, S.J. (1536–1612) was a theologian, religious apologist and writer of some consequence.

or commandment of love. This vital commandment is truly found at the center of human life, and it must be carried out in its entirety.

Youth enjoys certain privileges in this regard, but also has special duties. This commandment must penetrate to the very depths of our young people. It must shape your convictions and give direction to your actions and objectives. This is necessary, because life will be a test. In the course of your lives you will see what remains of that commandment of love, which must therefore penetrate into your young souls and hearts as clear truth, and as the incomparable ideal and principle according to which we must live our lives and without which human life in its various dimensions loses value.

We can understand this from different perspectives.

As twentieth-century men and women who have lived through terrifying periods of hatred, we can more easily appreciate this commandment in its great historical dimensions. The monstrous explosion of hatred, hostility and human destruction brought about by a terrible absence and negation of love, makes us realize its immense value.

There are other dimensions of human life in which the principle or commandment of love can and must be observed. We can see it when we study our social life. Wherever there is love, social bonds are strengthened, and wherever it is not found, they disintegrate—and this applies in a special way to the more fundamental bonds. We can see it when we suffer from the breakdown of those fundamental social bonds which link one person to another, those bonds which give form to human life from the cradle, or from birth itself, onwards, and which people are carefully taught from the very outset, as the highest good on earth. These are the bonds which in time enter into our professional life, our relationships with our work colleagues and our neighbors, and our social and political relations; they enter into the whole life of society, the nation and the state.

We must all realize that we are to a significant degree responsible for the construction of everything which exists today and will exist tomorrow, since it depends in large measure on the way in which we accept the commandment of love.

The commandment of love can—and, indeed, must—be linked to the need for commitment and the need to struggle. We can see this in the life of Christ himself: Christ loved and struggled. Struggle cannot be separated from love; struggle as an end in itself cannot be imposed on people or society, because it will give rise to the painful processes of man's destruction of man. If the life of society is systematically separated from the principle of love, in the place of noble competition we shall find things like ambitious career-orientation, and in place of an appreciation of the value of the person we shall find some anonymous self-interest and self-seeking.

"A new commandment I give to you, that you love one another" (John 13:34). This commandment applies at all times and in all places and in every dimension of life.

Now, my dear brothers and sisters, my dear young friends, take a look at life! Examine yourselves! And absorb into the depths of your young souls the commandment of love with all its great value and creative significance. There are many types of weakness and pitfall which can lead to its destruction in your souls and in social life. On the other hand, our task as Christians living on this earth is first and foremost to work for the victory of love.

Love contains a further affirmation or guarantee of the whole of human life, and to some degree also the guarantee that Christ is within each one of us. Did the Lord not say this when he described the scene of the Last Judgment? He stated it very clearly: "I was hungry and you gave me food, I was thirsty and you gave me drink, I was a stranger and you welcomed me, I was naked and you clothed me, I was sick and you visited me, I was in prison and you came to me" (Matthew 25:35–36). He identifies himself with each individual person. It is he who is received or refused in each person we receive or refuse; and it is he who wants—and is able—to release love in each person.

Saint John of the Cross wrote these profound words: "At the end of your life, you will be judged by your love."

If you believe what I am telling you, your practical task is to pay constant attention to the overriding question of how you can make the commandment of love the real center of your own lives.

Love has another side to it, in that it is closely linked to our human vocation. This is why, when we watch over a boy or girl, right from the time of elementary school we keep a careful eye on their preferences, so that later on we can be sure that their individual choice is in accordance with these preferences.

However, it has a still deeper significance, inasmuch as the person moves in the direction in which love calls him. How else can one explain a nun's vocation? Here is a girl, apparently just like her friends; maybe, again like her friends, she took part in the graduation dance and joined in in various recreation activities; but one day without any warning she asks to be admitted to the novitiate. And what will she do for the rest of her life? She will do what we often see other sisters doing here in Cracow: from six in the morning till ten at night, she will climb up and down flights of stairs, caring for the sick whom nobody else bothers about, because they have been sent home from hospitals to families which often are not able to look after them. And this nun will be joyful and content throughout it all: she is the promised bride and has chosen a much greater love. It is always striking how the voice of the Bridegroom echoes, blotting out everything else and bringing the bride to follow him.

And how can we explain the vocation of the young man who was thinking seriously of simple human married love and a family and who suddenly realizes that this type of love cannot satisfy him?

It is a force or, rather, a Person which calls them. It is that invisible Bridegroom who leads your young friends to enclose themselves behind the gates of Carmel for the rest of their lives. I sometimes go to visit them, and I must confess that it is difficult to find more cheerful people.

However, this is not what I want to discuss now. I want to devote the rest of this talk to that aspect of love which reveals itself in most people, in line with that fundamental truth stated at the beginning of the book of Genesis: "God created man; . . . male and female created he them; . . . therefore a man leaves his father and his mother and cleaves to his wife, and they become one flesh" (Genesis 1:27; 2:24). These phrases, which are found right at the beginning of the Bible, are of special significance, and are part of what is sometimes known as the protogospel, rather as if it comprised a prototype of the Good News proclaimed by Christ our Lord.

When the Lord dealt with this subject in his teaching, he simply repeated the words of the protogospel, adding: "What God has joined together, let no man put asunder" (Matthew 19:6). How wonderful! You will no doubt read books about love and you will also study this subject. You may even write about it. But, believe me, you will always return with enthusiasm to those simple but fundamental words of the protogospel and the Gospel. They express everything: the whole truth about human life, about that dual complementarity the Creator has given us in the human person, and about the wealth which comes from that two-fold nature and which is expressed in the whole person—in the body and psyche, soul and senses, affections and, lastly, vocation. It is this richness, this complex of values which provides the basis for what we call love—love between engaged couples, love between man and wife, or love *tout court.*

It is also true that since the time those fundamental words were written and those fundamental laws proclaimed, this very simple but deep view and wealth have been understood, illustrated, studied, explained and interpreted in various different ways.

However, all this wealth is very often threatened from a number of different quarters. The threat can undoubtedly come directly from our own weakness, but it does often come from a broad range of other sources, springing from our way of thinking, our scale of values, and our social system.

While I am speaking, my thought turns to all my listeners who have in their lives traveled the path which leads to that union, or human "we," which was defined by the Creator at the beginning of human history, and in particular to those among you who are already experiencing married life or are preparing for it, but who are also, like all of us, children of the present age. The whole system of interpreting and dealing with these issues as found in European society and, more specifically, in our Polish society, in this day and age, will already be impinging on your consciousness. It must be pointed out that a whole set of very serious misapprehensions and errors is entailed in this system of interpretation, evaluation, and what we can call proposal or suggestion.

The principle of divorce, or the dissolution of marriage, has become firmly rooted in our own Polish life. "What

God has joined together, let no man put asunder." These are the words of Christ, and they are the words the Church echoes. People—or society—have created another principle, apparently in the name of freedom. Do they really think that freedom can exist in opposition to love? And can it be true freedom if it is opposed to love and to union?

Union, or communion, must be carefully nurtured. We must create the right conditions for this communion and for the formation and development of human love, rather than creating that illusory freedom which costs people so dear and which is normally paid for not only by husband and wife but by others as well.

We are coming to have more and more homes *for* children, instead of homes *with* children. Is this really social progress? Is this really the right way to plan our future?

Then we have the question of the brutalization of human life. God said, "You shall not kill" (Exodus 20:13), in other words, do not kill another person. From the moment of conception there is another person. God told us not to kill, and we allow this to be done!

This inevitability has a lethal effect for the social conscience. On the other hand, there is also of necessity a material price to be paid. All the contraceptive propaganda which does not encourage people to enjoy their married life in a responsible fashion will have its price.

People want to see the person as some sort of object or instrument, but this is simply not possible when we are dealing with the act of love. Let us put it more plainly and state that this is simply a renunciation of love! If we examine our psyches and consciences, we shall maybe see that love has given way to instinct and libido.

All this will inevitably affect the relationship between the generations. If the next generation—that of our children— grows up with the knowledge that there are certain meth-

ods of contraception and abortion, at a certain moment they
will realize that they could in fact have been destroyed by
their own parents with these same means.

These are very frightening and serious considerations.

The divine law is wise. The law of love is demanding,
and we cannot evade its requirements. They must be accepted and respected.

My dear children, I am not talking about this in order to
offend anybody, but because I am saddened; however, I
also draw hope from the deep faith of your noble young
souls, from your desire for true love, and from your faith in
the words of Christ and in his sacrament.

Matrimony is a great sacrament for us Christians, and it
is a holy thing. It places two people—a man and a woman—in the presence of God himself, before whom they
make vows of love, sincerity and mutual fidelity, and these
attitudes should shape their whole lives. There is something
wonderful in these marriage vows, and we must be very
careful about one single aspect: that they are made with as
much commitment as possible, so that the couple's hearts
and wills (in other words, the whole of themselves as persons) may hold steadfastly to them.

The Church teaches love, that love which Christ
preached and which constitutes the human community or
"we" and makes it authentic. Two beings enter into life
united and bound together in this way, not only by faith,
but by their own decision and will and by their vows. There
is something very great in this! And this greatness must be
protected and developed. It must also be prayed for without
ceasing, because the way to approach it is through work
and prayer.

However, there is one basic precondition: we must not
deny the underlying basis of this greatness but must see hu-

man and Christian marriage as Christ instituted it in accordance with the words of his Father.

This is your task, my dear children. It is the main task and fundamental apostolate of lay people in the Church, and expresses the human and Christian message of every man and woman who, marrying and living out their marriage, form a family.

The Church teaches us about our responsibility as parents, and this teaching is of great value. The concepts of responsible fatherhood and "conscious" motherhood must never be confused. Responsible fatherhood never allows that which is often heralded as conscious motherhood. Paternity first and foremost means responsibility for the other, for the nearest person and for the new human being to whom life is given. Responsible fatherhood also has a broader sense, inasmuch as we are responsible for society as a whole, since, as we know, society is made up of people and its future depends on them. In the same way, the future of Poland is bound up, in the final analysis, with the attitudes of couples and families in our society.

All I have said today is by way of being a brief indication. I know that conferences and congresses are held on this subject, so I am not going to discuss the various more specific questions which have already been raised in the course of these meetings.

In conclusion, I want once more to remind you all that Christ is the exemplar and witness of human community. In the first place he is the witness of that basic, primordial community which has the greatest future and on which everything to come depends: the communion of man and woman, husband and wife, and, even before this, boy and girl—maybe like you, my dear children. Christ has been the witness of your communion as it grows, from the first quickenings of your hearts and the successive development of this love, up to and including the decision and the sacrament, and this will continue for the rest of your lives.

May Christ be the witness of every union right to the very end, and may he testify to this before his Father!

We end our meditation each day with a prayer, and today, too, we shall conclude by praying. It will be very like a litany, inasmuch as it refers back to the various subjects touched on in this reflection.

We ask the Mother of God for love. Every mother is, and must be, the heart of the family. Thus, as the Mother of Christ she brings us true love, that love which receives its name from God and which has its only source in him. She brings this love to us and implants it within the various dimensions of our very selves. So let us pray: *Ave Maria.* . . .

Amen

4. The Sacrament of Forgiveness

Today we shall talk about the sacrament of Penance. It will be, perhaps, a good thing at the outset to call to mind the old precept of the Church which enjoins us to confess at least once a year and to receive communion at Easter.

This instruction naturally enough bears the marks of its historical origins. It was formulated after that period of fervor for frequent communion and of deep feeling for Penance, which marked the first centuries of Christianity. Despite these origins, insofar as it is a precept of the Church it constitutes a sure instruction for us too and retains its value even in the present century, when frequent communion has become the norm. The precept of the Church simply gives the minimum requirement.

We must therefore bear in mind not only the precept but above all the reasons behind it. What are the benefits deriving from these great sacraments of the Easter season? I want to meditate on the sacrament of Penance today, and then we can consider the Eucharist tomorrow.

I remember a conversation I had before the war with a writer several decades my senior, whose literary work was not always easy to follow. If one examined his writings it was difficult to decide whether he was a believer or not. However, in the course of that conversation, he began to talk about confession, and if I remember clearly after so many years, he said something like this: "What a splendid institution confession is! If it didn't exist, we'd have had to invent it. It's so necessary to people!" When he said this he may have been thinking of the various expedients which people have invented, in a certain sense to fill the vacuum left by confession, and which act as sort of substitutes for it. These methods of treatment are even more widely known and used today; they form part of psychotherapy. These practices tend progressively to free the conscious, and more importantly the subconscious, of everything which has accumulated there. This takes place in the course of special sessions under the guidance of the psychotherapist, who asks questions, thus allowing the patient to start objectivizing what makes him suffer and what disturbs him. We know that, even outside psychotherapy, being able to talk about the cause of our suffering (even in the case of some quite minor sickness) always provides some relief. However, in my opinion, we are dealing here with two elements: in the first place, the objectivization of what has gathered in our conscious or unconscious in an irrational manner; and, in the second place, the expression of all this. This is what in a certain sense liberates us; at least the object of psychotherapy is to free the person from what is stagnating in his mind. We are clearly dealing with liberation or exoneration in a purely subjective sense.

It would be difficult to compare this practice with confession, even if they do have certain elements in common. In confession we do of course feel the need to express what is on our minds and what is upsetting and disturbing our consciences. However, the similarity is only partial, and we shall see this in the course of the explanation I want to give.

Let us begin with the most important aspect, which is one that does not exist in psychotherapy and which is, on the other hand, the essential element of the sacrament of Penance. Here we must begin with the words of our Lord

Jesus himself. When he gave his Apostles the power of this sacrament, he told them: "If you forgive the sins of any, they are forgiven" (John 20:23). The essential element is that of objective remission and not that of subjective experience of absolution and of liberation from what we have within us. The vital point is objective remission.

The Lord said, "If you forgive the sins of any . . . ," but before this he had said, "Receive the Holy Spirit." And this first expression, which is so solemn and pneumatological (please excuse me if I use theological terminology) indicates the objective significance of remission. Moreover, throughout his ministry Jesus had been preparing them for these words and this mission.

Let us consider the various occasions in our Lord's public life when he himself forgave sins. Let us recall the occasion when they brought the paralyzed man to him, and the first thing he said was: "Take heart, my son; your sins are forgiven" (Matthew 9:2). This provoked at least interior indignation in his listeners. The Lord saw into their minds and asked them: "Which is easier, to say, 'Your sins are forgiven,' or to say, 'Rise and walk'? But that you may know that the Son of man has authority on earth to forgive sins"—he then said to the paralytic—"Rise, take up your bed and go home."

This was a wonderful moment, and through this event and many others the Lord prepared his Apostles for the mission they were to receive from his own lips after his resurrection: "Receive the Holy Spirit. If you forgive the sins of any, they are forgiven; if you retain the sins of any, they are retained." This is thus the essential element of the sacrament of Penance, which is really the sacrament of absolution.

In order to understand the objective significance of absolution, we must first of all bear in mind that we are dealing not solely with something negative which has insinuated itself into the conscious or unconscious of the patient, but with the objective reality of sin. Absolution is in fact what removes somebody from that real situation of sin.

Here the model of psychotherapy can provide us with only a partial parallel. In my opinion there are other much simpler and more suitable models. What happens in the sacrament of Penance is very similar to what takes place between people, and this can maybe be seen most clearly in the relationship between parents and children. For example, a mother tells her child: "Go and apologize to your father, because you've been very naughty." The child goes and does this, and his father forgives him. This is not some sort of convention, but is something very real. His father's forgiveness relieves even a very young child's mind and conscience of a real weight or sense of guilt. Thus, in order to understand the objective significance of absolution, we must realize the objective context of guilt and sin. What we read throughout the Bible, throughout divine revelation, from the first to the last page, about the objective facts of sin is of capital importance; the choice of sin itself began with the first fall of our earliest forebears. This choice is clearly presented as a moral evil which is committed against a Person—and not against just anyone, but against the unique Someone.

When God created the world he imprinted in it an order which is comprehensible and decipherable to mankind, and when we violate this order we are aware that we have offended God. Some people will see all this as very depressing. However, the awareness of moral evil and sin, clearly and explicitly defined, and also the knowledge of whom it offends against, gives us a great advantage. Unknown sin or sin which we do not see clearly, and sin where the conditions make it easy to blur it over or mask it, are much worse. We are living in such a period and under such conditions, whereas the Bible, on the other hand, describes a very clear situation.

The awareness of sin, with which the person knows before whom and towards whom he is guilty, is an indispensable precondition for obtaining the objective value of forgiveness. This is because he against whom the sin is committed and who is therefore offended is also the Father who has the power to forgive it.

This is not a question of freeing the human conscience of certain negative contents but of a new relationship, with, on the one hand, the objective reality of sin which weighs the conscience down, and, on the other, he against whom we have committed the sin and who has the power to absolve and free us from it. This new relationship is a great gift. The word *Gospel* means Good News, which is why I believe that it concerns above all this factor, this reality, this revelation.

People often claim that moral evil comes solely from the violation of some social good, and that evil and guilt consist of this violation. In these cases society avenges its rights and punishes the guilty person. This is right and just, so far as it goes, but it does not get to the root of the problem or resolve it in depth. In fact, a certain number of acts, although they are truly sins, in no way violate the social order in its visible structure. So how can they be expiated? Society obviously pursues its own rights and metes out justice to those who are guilty of infringing them.

In certain groups and societies, something like Christian penance takes place, in which, in accordance with certain norms, the guilty person must acknowledge his guilt and confess it before others, demonstrating his repentance and humbling himself. Humility has its place in the sacrament of Penance, and we shall talk of this in due course. However, in the sacrament this aspect has a different and much more delicate meaning; it is a question of humbling oneself before the Father and his sacred power. When a person humbles himself publicly before other people, can he feel as if he were humbling himself and confessing his guilt before the Absolute, especially when the very basis of his guilt is changeable, so that today one thing is right and tomorrow something else? And often the people before whom such guilt is confessed appear to be as guilty (if not more so) themselves.

After these considerations, let us return to the crux of the issue: forgiveness. God forgives. Indeed, God wants to forgive. The question is: which road leads to the forgiveness which has its source in God himself? Forgiveness is obviously always a free act and an expression of love. If a child asks his father's forgiveness, and his father says, "I forgive you," and kisses him on his forehead, love is being expressed in this gesture; the freedom and spontaneity of forgiveness are being expressed, and these are in fact characteristics of love. We know quite well that true forgiveness, which is a pure act of love or mercy, must be in harmony with justice, so that in a certain sense it is not possible to forgive "gratuitously." Forgiveness cannot be given without some guarantee and the person cannot be absolved of sin without a guarantee; there must be a guarantee for such an action. So what type of guarantee does God give for the forgiveness he offers us? His own love and mercy. This guarantee has a very specific and historical expression. God has shown mankind the price of his forgiveness, and the price of this divine forgiveness is called redemption.

The Son of God became man, and through his life and death he rendered justice to God's holiness, creating a sort of platform of justice in that merciful work. He brought justification to each person for each human sin, and he paid for this personally. In one of the psalms we find a sort of summary of Christ's message of redemption and justification. With prophetic inspiration, the psalmist wrote: "Burnt offering and sin offering thou hast not required. Then I said: 'Lo, I, *God*, come . . . to do thy will.' "* "Lo, I come." And we know how he comes, how God the Son takes on a body and assumes human nature and life. The whole of his life is redemption, but this is true in a special way of his passion and death. So we see how, after the Last Supper, Jesus went to the Mount of Olives, and even now, so many centuries later, we can still hear his conversation with his Father. We have just heard the words of the psalmist, "Lo, I come (with my whole being) . . . to do thy will, O Father." And now in the Garden of Gethsemane we hear the words of a man, "If it be possible, let this cup pass from me" (Matthew 26:39), and, immediately afterwards, "Nevertheless, not as I will, but as thou wilt." So simple. Without even the support of those who were closest to him, those three favorite disciples, who had fallen asleep instead.

Thus, the whole breadth of Christ's spiritual passion is revealed to us. We see how he, the Son of God, is truly man, and we also see how the divinity of his action does not mask the human effort of what he has undertaken, but instead throws it into relief. If there had been no Garden of Gethsemane we should not have been able to understand Christ's passion in its entirety. We should have been able to list the sufferings entailed, but the Garden of Gethsemane indicates their depth and reveals the mystery of the God-Man on his way to his death. We can say that, although it only lasted a brief ten hours, Christ's passion in a certain way sums up all possible suffering, be it physical, psychological or spiritual.

He was disappointed by his disciples, and betrayed and

---

*The author here makes reference to Psalm 40:7–9, interpreting it in the manner of Hebrews 10:5–10.

denied by the very closest of them. He was disappointed by the crowd, from which he could rightfully have expected gratitude, but which enthusiastically accepted his unjust condemnation instead. He was subjected to a terrible scourging, and then had a crown of thorns placed on his head. He was treated as an object to be traded for a murderer, after which sentence was passed—a sentence which even the judge was convinced was unjust. He carried the cross, stumbling beneath its weight, and finally he was crucified.

In recent times an effort has been made to reconstruct, so far as possible, the passion of Christ and his physical sufferings from a medical viewpoint. However, nobody can in any way enter into the depths of that passion, and nobody will be able to discover or reveal the inner dimension of the sufferings of the Man who was the Son of God. The prayer in the Garden of Gethsemane gives us a glimpse of this mystery, and the words spoken from the cross are closely linked to that prayer. Jesus addressed his Father, saying, "Father, forgive them, for they know not what they do" (Luke 23:34), but also, "My God, my God, why hast thou forsaken me?" (Matthew 27:46). All the most famous theologians of every age have stopped short in the face of this heart-rending cry. Lastly, he said, "Father, into thy hands I commit my spirit" (Luke 23:46), but, immediately before that, "It is finished" (John 19:30).

What had been finished? Christ knew the meaning of what he did, the actions of his life and his message. And when he said, "It is finished," he was referring to the fulfillment of the work of human redemption. The mystery of human justification before God—the foundation and the path for the remission of sins by God himself—is enclosed in that work.

This path for the remission of sins by God himself requires a parallel path on the part of human beings: consciousness of sin, but above all faith that only the Father, with the power of his fatherly forgiveness, can effectively remove us from this sin.

If we believe this, our faith must in some special way participate in the mystery of Christ's redemption. It is this union which is the basis of the sacrament of Penance, which has a principally divine structure; and it is in this divine structure that we find what is human.

We know about the human structure of the sacrament of Penance. We learned about it when we were children preparing for our first confession and first communion. Our teachers told us about the so-called conditions for the sacrament: examination of conscience, act of contrition, integral confession of sin, firm purpose of amendment, and performance of the penance imposed—and we all had to know them by heart.

However, knowing and reciting them was not enough; we had to be able to put them into practice even the first time. This may have been difficult for some of us as young children, and often we would ask our mothers to help us make our examination of conscience. In any case, this whole childhood experience affected us deeply, and was in some way the source of what would—and should—make up the framework and dynamism of the sacrament of Penance in every confession in every period of our lives.

When we go to confession frequently, everything is easier. On the other hand, when it is less frequent, it becomes more difficult and less objective, so that it can take on a mainly subjective character. The basic objective elements are the examination of conscience, the actual confession of our sins, and the reception of sacramental absolution.

As we grow older we therefore realize the significance of the act of contrition and the firm purpose of amendment, and of the interior disposition and commandment in question. The ancient Greeks and the Christians called this *met-anoia*, and we find this word in the Bible. *Metanoia* means a change of spirit, or spiritual transformation. We know how much such a transformation can cost, bound up, as it is, with interior effort. Sometimes people give up going to confession, precisely because they are afraid of this effort of the will. This is very foolish of them.

The sacrament of Penance flows from a great love and was bought at a high price—a price which Jesus Christ has paid! However, each of us must pay it too, in proportion to his or her own human capacity. It must be paid with the interior effort of conversion, which brings liberation; and this liberation is not only subjective, on the conscious level, but also gives us true freedom.

Do not fear that effort! Make it! It is wonderfully creative! God knows how he made us and what he can expect of us. He knows that we must challenge and be challenged in order to enter into possession of ourselves and not be a passive field where things "happen" and over which passing winds blow; but in order to be a person we must conquer ourselves with constant sacrifice.

The difficult thing about the sacrament of Penance is the effort of conversion, pain and resolution. This is equivalent to only a small fraction of the redemptive effort of Jesus Christ. If you are afraid and hesitant, then think of the fact that in this interior effort you will be closer to him and he to you. We do know that various other people helped him carry his cross.

Then there is the actual confession of sins. This is not a matter of describing or declaring them (which would not go deep enough), but of *confessing* them. Here I am, I've come to admit the truth about myself and to tell it to another person, who is separated from me and from what I am revealing, not only by the screen of the confessional, but also by the seal of confessional secrecy.

It must be admitted that this too can give rise to a problem. Humiliation is present, but we must be very careful not to revel in our guilt while confessing it.

"If you forgive the sins of any, they are forgiven; if you retain the sins of any, they are retained." This is what Christ told his Apostles. He gave this power to the Church and to precise people in it—the Apostles—and the power comes to us from them. The priest who sits in the confessional has received this power from them, through his own bishop.

Today, in accordance with the teachings of the Council, the social aspect of sin is emphasized—social in the sense of the Church. Sometimes penitential services are held in which the accent is placed on prejudice and on the harm sin does to the Church, the People of God, the Mystical Body of Christ.

We know that purification is needed on our path to God, and we also know that purgatory exists among the "last things." In the path to God, which is also the path to eternal life after death and judgment, there is purgatory, in other words, the need for purification through reparatory suffering. This is the way the mystery of redemption and justification by Christ works. We must enter into this deep mystery, which is both divine and human.

My dear listeners, a spiritual retreat helps us to prepare for the sacrament of Penance, and this is why I am devoting a great deal of attention to the subject. However, I am well aware that words are not enough and that prayer is needed—the prayer of each of us, communal prayer, the prayer of the whole Church, for all Christians who are living the Lenten season.

Let us take part in this prayer. Each day the Church raises

prayer for the conversion of sinners, and each day it prays to receive a fruitful celebration of the sacrament of Penance in this period. We too pray that our participation in this retreat may be crowned by confession, by a deep experience of the sacrament of Penance.

Each day we end our reflections with a communal prayer. Joint recitation of the act of repentance which we recite in the Holy Mass will best echo today's reflection: "I confess to Almighty God, and to you, my brothers and sisters. . . ."

Amen

5. The Eucharist

"Receive communion during the Easter season."

Today I want to return to this precept of the Church on the subject of Penance and the Eucharist. The expression "to receive communion" is very beautiful. Sometimes we also say that we "approach holy communion," and in this second expression—but maybe even better in the first one—holy communion is seen in an objective way, as sacrament and sign.

We all know the form of this sign: bread and wine, in the context of the whole bloodless sacrifice, from the offertory and the consecration through to communion itself.

We say that communion means simply union, but it can also mean community. The word *communio*, which we have been using frequently since Vatican II, cannot be properly translated into Polish. Holy communion simply means union, and therefore when people say, "I am receiving the Lord Jesus," they are expressing themselves correctly. Jesus is a person; he is the Divine Person, who also became man through the mystery of the Incarnation and is therefore an historical person, a person whom we can receive.

If we look at the question from this angle, we almost at once see the second element of this encounter or union-communion. We can therefore state clearly that at communion not only do I receive the Lord, but he also receives me. If we limit ourselves exclusively to the sign aspect, I receive the species of bread, or of bread and wine. However, if, through the sign, we come to the reality of the Eucharist— the reality of communion—then we must realize that here we have two people in one another's presence: Our Lord and me. We can even say that it is he who first receives me, allowing me to come to him when I receive him.

All this obviously goes hand in hand with a process of growing awareness and understanding, which takes place within the person in the following way: "If I am able to receive Our Lord, this means that my state is such that he too can allow me to come to him and can receive me."

The Eucharist is the greatest sacrament of our faith, and everything else is concentrated in it. Our Lord is present in it as Man, Son of God, and Son of Mary; he is present thanks to the power of the words he spoke and, as a result of the institution, he is present under the species which he himself chose as sign of his presence. We know that all this took place during the Last Supper when those species were quite naturally on the table to be shared between those who were eating with him. The words the Apostles heard him say were completely new and full of deep significance. Speaking of the bread, Christ said: "This is my body which is given for you." He then took the cup of wine and said: "This is the cup of my blood which is shed for you" (Luke 22:19–20). This took place on Holy Thursday, but his words already referred to the events of Good Friday.

The next day it became clear that his real body—the one he had received from his virgin mother—was to be condemned to death and his real blood shed. At that point the truth of those words spoken in the upper room the previous day became clear and certain—just as certain as they are every time that we follow Christ's express instructions and transubstantiation takes place, and we say, "Christ has died." These words which we speak today have been enriched by two thousand years of tradition, but when they were spoken for the first time by Christ's disciples and Apostles, they still had their immediate, original freshness.

These two events took place at the same time, parallel to one another, the first being, so to speak, concretized in the second. Jesus instituted the sacrament of his death, and the next day he gave himself up to death. Then the disciples celebrated this sacrament, while the living event was still fresh in their minds—the event which is referred to in the words, "This body which is given; this blood which is shed," and which confirmed the truth of these words. And we go on to say: "Christ is risen."

Let us reflect on how Christ's Apostles and disciples, who had already received the sacramental presence of the Eucharist must have been affected by all the events which took place after his death and resurrection, when he appeared to them when they were gathered in the upper room and allowed them to touch his body, which was still real, although different from before his passion. "Touch me, and see; for a spirit has not flesh and bones as you see that I have" (Luke 24:40).

In the same period the Eucharist was already developing in the first Christian group, that first community of Christ's Apostles and disciples, among whom was his mother, who had given him his body. Today we still repeat: "Christ has died. Christ is risen. Christ will come again." With these words and in this way, each time we take part in the Eucharist, we draw near to the key moments of our salvation— the events of Holy Thursday and Good Friday, and then Easter, the day of the resurrection—which for us are always the culminating points of the liturgical cycle.

The Eucharist is the great mystery of our faith. In it, Christ is truly present; and in it, the constant marvelous exchange takes place which began to take place in the human race through him and in him. The true God, the Son of God, took on human nature; the true God, the Son of God, endowed man with his divinity. The Father gave mankind divinity through his Son, and the Son obtained for mankind the coming of the Holy Spirit, whose work is sanctification, or grace. Every living person, every one of us, becomes a real participant in the divine nature, a participant in divinity.

That marvelous transformation takes place which does not stop on the surface of our humanity, but reaches the very essence of our nature, making it divine. "He gave them power to become children of God" (John 1:12). These words were written by Saint John, who also said, in another place: "We are called children of God; and so we are" (1 John 3:1). These are not just words, but are the reality; this marvelous exchange, which began in the mystery of the Incarnation inasmuch as "the Word was made flesh" (John 1:14), continues to take place in each person. Each communion is like a step toward the fulfillment of what began in the mystery of the Incarnation, a step toward bringing it about in each individual—in me and in you. "God is able from these stones to raise up children to Abraham" (Matthew 3:9), Christ said on one occasion. God can carry out that work of sanctification and of our transformation into his children through grace in many ways which are unfathomable to us.

We also know for certain that he carries out our sanctification through the Eucharist, working in a sacramental, and in a certain sense visible, manner. Obviously we do not see the mystery of what takes place in the person's soul, elevating his whole spiritual essence to the supernatural dignity of children of God. On the other hand, what we can see in the Eucharist are the species of bread and wine. And, thanks to the faith which has its source in the upper room, we can discover the origin of this process, which takes place in each person throughout the whole Church.

Admirabile commercium—"marvelous exchange." In a certain way we also bring our humanity here, too. We give our humanity to him who wants to give us his divinity in sacramental communion, that mystery of faith. When we gaze on this mystery with the eyes of faith, then its fundamental effects on the eschatological level manifest themselves.

I have already referred to this level twice before: the first time when I spoke of death and judgment, and the second when I spoke of purgatory. Today I want to complete discussion of this subject.

God wants to unite us with himself, and this is of vital importance for each person.

The first time we considered two possible alternatives: either death is the end of everything, or the person matures toward death, moving toward judgment. At that point we stopped.

Now that we are speaking of the Eucharist and of God the Son's uniting himself with us, we must go further. We must say that the person—and man is a person—is called to union. This is his most important characteristic, and this is why he was created.

The Creator is also Father, and his paternity is expressed in the fact that he wants union between man and himself. Eucharistic communion prepares us for this and is already true union with God. Receiving the Lord means true union with God, and at this point the person enters into the eschatological perspective. You receive the Lord Jesus, so that you are starting on this union which is your vocation and final destination. We of course know that, in the final analysis, the choice between union or refusal is necessarily present in every human action.

You must obviously realize that I am talking here of what in biblical and catechetical language are known as heaven and hell. Maybe our image of these two realities has been clouded sometimes by additional elements drawn from the imagination. Let us concentrate on the heart of the matter— the choice between union and refusal, union with God or refusal of God. Eucharistic communion is the beginning of union, and it guides the person living on earth toward union with God; this is its eschatological significance and we must always remember this fact.

We should always bear in mind the whole breadth of our faith and not try to narrow it down. This global, overall perspective of our faith can explain everything about the human person in his entirety. The Eucharist is thus initiation or entry into that perspective of the eschatological condition which is the most important of all and which goes beyond the thought and perception faculties of our human condition: "What no eye has seen, nor ear heard, nor the heart of man conceived" (1 Corinthians 2:9).

The Eucharist is the sacrament of faith. Moreover eucharistic communion is also the sacrament of those who live on this earth, the people of God, who are on pilgrimage toward the final truth, toward union with the Father, toward the fulfillment of the Kingdom of God. However, this pilgrimage takes place here, through and on this earth.

The Eucharist is suited to this pilgrim state in a wonderful way: it is real food. A person on a journey who begins to tire must try to gain new strength; this is simply common sense. There is only goodness in the Eucharist, which is food. It is a gift, but it also entails certain conditions. This fact was clear even to the first Christian communities, and Saint Paul wrote about this, especially in his first letter to the Corinthians, a first-century apostolic community in which the people gathered together to participate in the Eucharist. Paul spoke very strongly: "Let each person examine himself, and so eat of the bread and drink of the cup" (1 Corinthians 11:28).

Let each person examine himself. In the Eucharist I receive Christ, but Christ also receives me, and this is where I must assume my responsibility, examining and testing myself. I must ask myself if he can receive, approve and accept me as I am. This is the ancient Christian tradition, and is in any case inevitable, since it is absolutely necessary to examine ourselves, measuring ourselves against these conditions and answering the questions: Can he accept me? Can he receive me?

Sometimes we shy away from these questions and look for some other way out. The expression, "I am not worthy," can be taken in a wrong sense. This is not a Christian attitude. The more conditions are imposed by Christ, the Eucharist and communion, the more commitment is required in their fulfillment. And the only authentically Christian attitude can be expressed as: I make an effort and do as much as I can. "Lord, I am not worthy to have you come under my roof, but only say the word, and my soul will be healed" (cf. Luke 7:6–7). This is the attitude of those who receive Christ and are aware that Christ too receives them in a certain way.

For us who are disciples of Christ, the Eucharist is still the center of the community. Right from the beginning, the Eucharist has always created community. This was the case at the Last Supper for the Apostles who were gathered around Christ, and this has been the case in every Christian community, just as it still is today. The eucharistic community has two dimensions. The first brings us to that focal point constituted by the Lord himself and his sacrament; the sacrament of his presence, of his body and blood, of his death and resurrection, is also the sacrament of our expectation. The second dimension is that of us in relation with one another; it is the dimension of the human community, which entails drawing near to one another, mutual union, co-operation, and forgiveness; it is the dimension of all those deep Gospel attitudes which should be seen in people who gather together around Christ.

We may sometimes feel that our parish life is not very communitarian and that we do not know one another; we know little of one another's concerns and worries, and we do not help one another. However, if the community exists around this unique focal point of Christ and his body and blood, then we see how defective this second dimension is. It is a good thing if we realize this, although it means that we are faced with a huge task, inasmuch as that community between people—the community of love of neighbor, of social love—must always be created by us. And this will always be the case until the end of time.

Saint Paul criticized the Corinthians for not observing the rules of this community, for this problem existed even then. And many people today write about it; those concerned in pastoral work discuss it, as we do too. It means that we are faced with a task. There is an explicit continuity or identity between that first eucharistic community of the upper room and the eucharistic communities of our times. Each parish community and each eucharistic gathering has its place in this continuity. In our case, this is undoubtedly true of our parish of university students, when they gather to take part in the liturgy of the word in a general sense, and in the eucharistic liturgy which, so to speak, flows from the liturgy of the word.

I wanted to speak about the Eucharist today, since this retreat will be brought to a conclusion tomorrow with a communitarian celebration of the Holy Mass, when we shall receive Holy Communion.

I should like us to bring today's reflection to a close with a short prayer, as we have been doing each day. However, I should like today's prayer to be an especially attentive meditation of the Way of the Cross, since today is Good Friday and this devotion is completely in tune with our retreat. Although this meditation will be longer than our other daily prayers, it will in fact be brief. We shall pause in reflection before each of the Stations of the Cross.

First Station: Jesus is condemned to death. Pilate says: "Behold the man." Jesus says: "I came into the world to bear witness to the truth." O Lord Jesus, who suffered for us, have mercy on us.

Second Station: Jesus carries the cross. "Sacrifices and offerings thou hast not desired, but a body hast thou prepared for me. Then I said, 'Lo, I have come to do thy will, O God.'" O Lord Jesus, who suffered for us, have mercy on us.

Third Station: Jesus falls for the first time. "Here is he who is set for the fall and rising of many." O Lord Jesus, who suffered for us, have mercy on us.

Fourth Station: Jesus meets his mother. "And a sword will pierce through your own soul also, that thoughts out of many hearts may be revealed." O Lord Jesus, who suffered for us, have mercy on us.

Fifth Station: Simon of Cyrene helps Jesus to carry his cross. "They compelled Simon of Cyrene to carry his cross." They *compelled* him . . . O Lord Jesus, who suffered for us, have mercy on us.

Sixth Station: Veronica wipes the face of Jesus. "You have done well; you have performed a good deed toward me; you did this for love." "Where your treasure is, there will your heart be also." O Lord Jesus, who suffered for us, have mercy on us.

Seventh Station: Jesus falls for the second time. "He was wounded for our transgressions; he was condemned for our malice. By his wounds we have been healed." God have mercy on us sinners. O Lord Jesus, who suffered for us, have mercy on us.

Eighth Station: Jesus meets the women of Jerusalem. "Do

not weep for me, but weep for yourselves and for your children." "Blessed are those who weep." Grant us the grace of sorrow for sin. O Lord Jesus, who suffered for us, have mercy on us.

Ninth Station: Jesus falls for the third time. "He emptied himself, and became obedient unto death." O Lord, grant me the grace of conversion. You who fell are placed for the fall and rising again. O Lord Jesus, who suffered for us, have mercy on us.

Tenth Station: Jesus is stripped of his garments. "Do you not know that your body is a temple?" "Blessed are the pure in heart, for they will see God." O Lord Jesus, who suffered for us, have mercy on us.

Eleventh Station: Jesus is nailed to the cross. "They have pierced my hands and feet; they have numbered all my bones; they divide my garments among them, and for my raiment they cast lots." Be merciful to us sinners. O Lord Jesus, who suffered for us, have mercy on us.

Twelfth Station: Jesus dies on the cross. "When I am raised up I shall draw all things to myself." "Father, forgive them, for they know not what they do." "My God, my God, why have you forsaken me?" "Father, into your hands I commend my spirit." Christ, into your hands I entrust my soul. O Lord Jesus, who suffered for us, have mercy on us.

Thirteenth Station: Jesus is taken down from the cross. "Mother, behold your son." "Holy Mary, Mother of God, pray for us sinners." O Lord Jesus, who suffered for us, have mercy on us.

Fourteenth Station: Jesus is placed in the tomb. "I am the resurrection and the life; whoever believes in me, even if he be dead, shall live forever." O Lord Jesus, who suffered for us, have mercy on us. Lord Jesus. . . .

Amen

6. Christ Within Us

The last day of our retreat coincides with the feast of the Annunciation, and in this last meditation I want to bring to a close our consideration of the Eucharist, linking it with today's liturgy.

When we listen carefully to God's word on the day of the Annunciation, we remember those words of the psalmist which we have already recalled a number of times this week: "Sacrifices and offerings thou hast not desired. . . . Then I said, 'Lo, I have come to do thy will, O God' " (Psalm 40:6–8). Saint Paul quotes these lines in his letter to the Hebrews (10:5–7). We know that they have a Christological and Messianic significance, and that they speak of the Incarnation, of what the Church remembers every year on the feast of the Annunciation: "But a body hast thou prepared for me"—this is what the Word, the Son of God, says to his Father, speaking of the moment in which he became man.

Today's Gospel reading, taken from Saint Luke, tells us of the event of the Incarnation of the Son of God, the eternal Word. The evangelist describes this event from the viewpoint of someone narrating an historical episode.

So let us return to Mary's conversation with the Archangel and hear the words with which he announced what was to take place within her if she gave her consent, and then let us hear her words of acceptance.

Today's liturgy shows us not only the moment of the Annunciation but also the event of the Incarnation, so that we have, so to speak, two different facets of the same event—from the perspective of the Son of God, the Word made flesh, and from that of the Virgin Mary, who becomes the mother of the Word, the mother of the Son of God, the mother of God, through the operation of the Holy Spirit. This is the focal point of today's liturgy.

Let me now move backwards in time from this event to the one which was so beloved of our Blessed Maximilian Kolbe. The moment he loved most especially in the mystery of Christ and Mary was not so much that of the Incarnation as that of the Immaculate Conception, which he saw as the beginning and basis of the whole mystery. When she revealed herself to Saint Bernadette at Lourdes, Mary would say, "I am the Immaculate Conception," and this means that her name and title are defined and have their basis in this event. In the fact of Mary's conception without original sin, Father Maximilian saw not only what we normally see in it, that is, liberation from original sin, but above all total openness to God and to all that comes from him. This total and unconditional openness to God and to everything divine was expressed by Mary, and it constituted the preparation for that moment when she would become the mother of God and when her virginal body would give the Son of God his temporal beginnings—that moment which is remembered by the Church on the feast of the Annunciation.

The Annunciation also has a eucharistic element. The Eucharist is the sacrament of the body and blood; it is *the* sacrament. It is thanks to Mary that the Son of God, Jesus Christ, makes this body and blood real. Together with his human nature, she also gave him his human body and blood, just as every mother gives flesh and blood to her own child. When she gave them to the Son of God she accepted in the fullest manner that marvelous exchange, that *admirabile commercium* we spoke of yesterday. She was filled with divinity in the most complete way, which is why the Archangel who came to her greeted her as "full of grace" (Luke 1:28). "Full of grace" means totally filled with God, sharing fully in divinity, in the divine nature. Then the angel called her "blessed."

We can thus say that the Annunciation is the prototype of every communion, of our every human and Christian communion. We receive God's gift, the gift of Christ, the Son of God, who, in the Eucharist and through communion, bears our humanity in its entirety, not excluding the elements of conversion, purification and amendment of life, mixed with a deep humility: "Lord, I am not worthy." In order for the event of the Annunciation to be a model for our communion, our Eucharist must be modelled on it.

Yesterday we spoke of the relationship between the mystery of the Incarnation and the Eucharist. Today our Eucharist is celebrated on the day when the Church lives the mystery of the Incarnation in a special way—the feast of the Annunciation. This is a most important feast, and the Church emphasizes this, celebrating it nine months before Christmas. The basic thread running through the liturgical year is always Mary, Mary blessed among women, Mary full of grace, Mary who has conceived, Mary who carries the Son of God in her womb, just as every mother carries her own child. "Blessed is the fruit of thy womb" (Luke 1:42).

From today onward and throughout the whole liturgical year, may Mary continue to stand out on the horizon of the Church and be a guideline and inspiration for our every communion, for each marvelous exchange which must take place between the human soul and the Son of God.

The Incarnation is the central and focal event in the history of human salvation, and all the paths of human salvation begin with it, going back into the past and stretching forward into the future. They go back into the past, right to mankind's beginnings, right back to the protogospel to which we have already referred a number of times in the course of this retreat. The first humans heard those words, that first Good News, after the fall. They heard those words directed against the tempter: she and her descendants would crush the serpent's head. "I will put enmity between you and the woman, and between your seed and her seed (Genesis 3:15). Even then, at the beginning of human history and the history of salvation, that event which we call the Incarnation of the Son of God had begun. This path leads us through the whole history of the people of God of the Old Testament, in which at intervals we glimpse the vision a prophet sees of what will take place at the right moment: "Behold, a virgin shall conceive and bear a son, and shall call his name Emmanuel" (Isaiah 7:14). Today this event is the joy of the Church. It was the joy of the people of God of the Old Testament, hundreds of years before the birth of Christ. The Incarnation thus leads us back into the past.

The mystery of the Incarnation is the highest moment in the order of salvation in human history, or, to put it another way, it is the culminating and focal point of the history of salvation.

However, our attention should be focused chiefly on those paths which project from the mystery of the Incarnation into the future toward our own times, through the early days of the Church and the history of the people of God of the New Testament, of whom we too have formed part for many centuries.

The Church lives the mystery of the Incarnation in unbroken continuity and sees itself as the extension of that mystery, taking this as the reason for its very existence. We are the people of God because God became one of us, became man, became the Man.

In our days, the Church has clear knowledge of this mystery: we just have to glance at the documents of the Second Vatican Council, especially the central one on the Church, in order to find evidence of this awareness. Today, in the context of the Eucharist, it will be helpful if we devote some consideration to the mind of the Church in modern times; this is particularly important in the eucharistic context, since the Eucharist continues to build up the Church in a special way.

The shared Eucharist which we are living today, this retreat communion, is a most important action in building up the Church.

So what is the mind of the Church today? What I tell you may seem like a repetition of my previous explanations, but I do think that it will be helpful to summarize certain aspects at the end of the retreat.

In my opinion, the mind of the Church today is composed of three elements. The first element is the dignity of the human person. Each person is unique and draws his whole greatness from being rooted in his relationship with God, because he was created in the image and likeness of God, and also from the fact that God himself has a special relationship with each individual person.

The mission of the Church is oriented to human dignity and greatness, and takes on a special significance in our times, when so many facts (and not just theories) militate against human dignity and greatness; these facts may or may not be close to us, and they may relate directly to our lives or to the life of the world.

This is the first element in the mind of the Church today, and the Second Vatican Council, in which I took part from the very first, gave particularly expressive evidence of this.

The second element in fact follows from the first. Man, who is a person, constantly experiences and lives out his own supernatural life within the community. This is an important point to bear in mind, in view of various erroneous opinions based on the religious individualism of the past. In the community of the people of God, the religious life always means participation. However, the community has different dimensions. The narrowest dimension is the family, but, as the primary and basic human community, it is also the most fruitful and fundamental one. This community, which can and should be the primordial community of persons *par excellence*, is the community in which there is both full interpersonal exchange between the persons (husband and wife, parents and children), and also a special possibility of sharing in the mystery of our salvation and in all the truths which express it and all the forces which bring it about.

The community of the people of God then expands and takes on many different aspects. Yesterday I began with the specific aspect it has assumed over the past centuries in this old church of Saint Anne in Cracow, that is, the community of university students. Each parish is a special community with specific tasks, because of the people of which it is composed.

The university environment is a highly intellectual one, and religious consciousness and moral maturity must be in line with this aspect. We must sincerely admit that intellectual circles—and I believe our country is not alone in this—do not express a moral maturity in proportion with their intellectual maturity. A vast effort must be made to correct this imbalance. University pastoral work is based on the fact that more is expected of those who have received more, so that the university congregation and environment should not provoke divisions in the ordinary congregation and parish environment, but should on the contrary revitalize them.

These different groups and communities of the people of God, who gather around their pastors, and through them gather around Christ in a dynamic manner, seek to bring about the fullness of the Christian life.

This is the Church, the Church in its global dimension and in each of its parts. Each part of this Church—each parish, each diocese, each individual church of the different countries—has the same life as the universal Church. This is not so much a sociological phenomenon as an element in a great mystery: the Church is always the same in each individual part and in its totality.

On many occasions during and after the Council, we had the opportunity of meeting the ancient middle eastern churches, which go back to apostolic times, and also the ancient churches of India, which began a little later. And then we also met with some very young chur hes, the bishop of one of which said that he was not even born into the Christian faith; this bishop had received baptism as an adult, and had then traveled along the road to the priesthood and the episcopate, taking on responsibility for the church of his own origin. There is a deep significance in these meetings: the reality of our identity in Christ, our evangelical identity that perdures despite human weaknesses and failings. It is the Christian identity of the one single Church.

This is the Church which is today rediscovering what unites it with all the other Christian communities. The vast ecumenical movement is the expression of union with all believers and also with people who profess other faiths. It is, lastly, the bond which links all people of good will. This is the image and mind of the Church today.

We must assimilate this "mind" or consciousness in the right way, because there are also certain false notions which may be met with in the process of assimilation.

I feel that the third and last element of which I want to

speak is very important for all of you who are listening to me.

The Second Vatican Council specifically mentioned and emphasized the vocation of each individual Christian, together with the importance of human dignity and of the fact that one's religious life is lived in community. Consciousness of the vocation of each Christian is a constitutive element and also a direct result of the vision we have of the Church today. We are in the Church, and this means that we are in Christ, which in turn means that, through him, each of us has a place in God's specific plans, in his intentions as they affect each one of us.

We must think in this way, and see ourselves from the viewpoint of the faith. The mind of the Church as we have acquired it and possess it today means that we must view ourselves, our life, our profession and our situation in this framework.

In the past the concept of vocation was maybe reserved solely to certain conditions of life and referred only to the priesthood or the religious life. But what if I were a lay person?

Today we are living a remarkable renaissance in our understanding of the vocation of the laity. For example, we may view the occupation of a doctor, an engineer, an attorney or a professor as a profession, but we will also see them as callings or vocations.

What exactly does this mean? It means that in everything you do in your life by way of professional training and education and pursuit of your career must also contribute to some good God wants for the world for which Christ sacrificed himself. In your life as a lay person you cannot ignore or neglect this dimension but must enter into it. This is a wonderful invitation; it is a call to enter into and find your own place in the broad and deep mind of the Church.

These are the three elements to which I wanted to draw your attention at the close of our meditations, particularly in the context of today's Eucharist and the great feast of the Annunciation, which is the feast of the first moment in the mystery of the Incarnation.

Saint Paul formulated a marvelous analogy for the mystery of the Incarnation of the body of Christ, calling the Church "the body of Christ." We often refer to it as the mystical body, and we could in a certain sense call it the social body.

The Council described the Church above all as the people of God, and if this concept is examined in depth we shall find that it contains the great Pauline analogy of the body of Christ. Indeed, everything we do, all our different vocations and our whole lives, are Christian existences which begin in the sacrament of Baptism, take shape in the sacrament of Confirmation, and are constantly reconstituted in the sacrament of Penance. Thus in an organic way all our Christian lives and vocations form one single body, in analogy with the body of Christ.

Let us return to what we said at the outset about how the Son of God was conceived in the womb of the Virgin Mary and how his body took shape in that womb in those blessed months of pregnancy. This is the image of the beginning. Now all those who participate in Christ through Baptism and the other sacraments, especially the Eucharist, must come to resemble that image. In the same way we are formed, united and integrated into the body of Christ, his mystical body. And the Eucharist is the focal point in this process. It is the best expression of the exchange between divinity and humanity, and brings this exchange about in its fullness. In and through it we men enter fully into the mystical body of Christ and give it its vitality.

It is very beautiful that we conclude our retreat by celebrating the Eucharist on the feast of the Annunciation, for the Eucharist has a deeply interior content, as we saw yesterday. In it we also find the second dimension—that of the people of God, of the mystical body of Christ, of all of us united in it through its one Master and Head. Christ himself showed this at the Last Supper, when he told his disciples (and us): "Abide in me, and I in you . . . for apart from me you can do nothing" (John 15:4–5).

This is a call to communion, and not merely occasional communion, but frequent communion, to the organic communion which constantly builds up the body of Christ. The *mystical* body of Christ is built up from the *sub specie* body of Christ.

We can—and must—think with immense gratitude of that first moment of the body of Christ on earth, that moment of the Incarnation, when "the Word became flesh" (John 1:14). We can and must think of that moment with immense gratitude to Mary. The Church, seeking to repay this debt of gratitude, honors her for having said, "Let it be to me according to your word" (Luke 1:38).

There is a true element of motherhood in the Eucharist, inasmuch as a mother feeds her children. Christ, who was born of the Virgin, Christ the Son of God who had her as mother, gives himself in this aspect of motherhood. The mother nourishes us also in the Eucharist.

And the Church sees Mary as its model; the Church, which refers to itself very humbly as "mother," experiences its motherhood more deeply when it can nourish every one of us. We are all nourished by this bread and wine. We are all formed and spiritually constituted by the Eucharist; especially when we receive our Lord in the Blessed Sacrament, the Church feels it is our mother, and then it turns its grateful gaze on that mother who gave flesh and blood to the Son of God.

My dear listeners, I want to thank you for your presence over these six days of communitarian union and recollection, prayer and interior work, in order to prepare ourselves as well as possible for this year's celebration of Easter, for the celebration of the paschal mystery which should provide further encouragement to faith and to that life which springs from it, and which must lead us to that victory given by faith, in accordance with Saint John's words: "This is the victory that overcomes the world, our faith" (1 John 5:4).

May we all share in this victory!

Amen